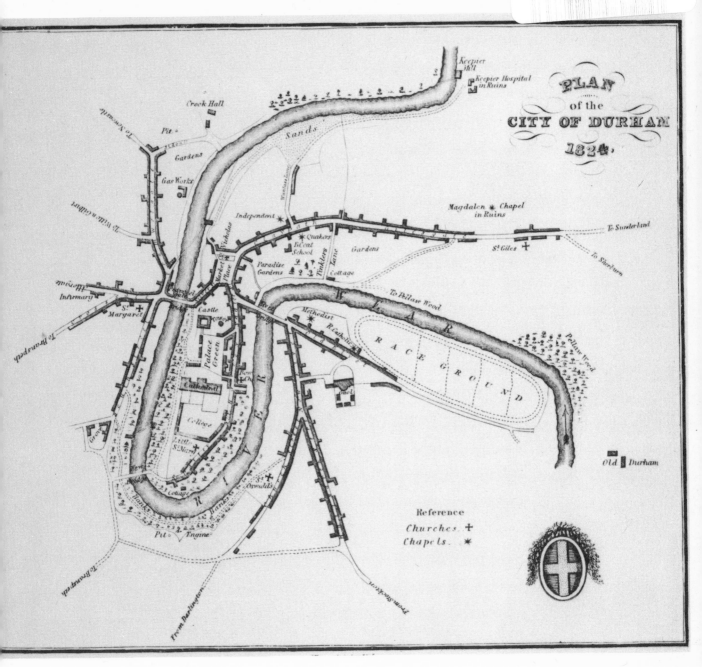

PLAN of the CITY OF DURHAM 1824.

Keeper Mill

Keeper Hospital in Ruins

Crook Hall

Pit

Gardens

Gas Works

Sands

To Newcastle

To Milton Gilbert

Independent

Magdalen Chapel in Ruins

To Sunderland

To Sherburn

Quakers

B. Coat School

Gardens

St Giles

Paradise Gardens

Tinklers Lane

Cottage

St Nicholas

Market Place

To Pelaw Wood

Infirmary

St Margaret

Castle

Tower

Methodist

R. Catholic

R A C E   G R O U N D

Pelaw Wood

To Brancepeth

Palace Green

Row Ch.

Cathedral

College

Pit

Engine

Little St Mary

Goal

To Brancepeth

Cottage

St Oswald's

Old Durham

From Darlington

From Stockton

Reference
Churches.....+
Chapels......*

THE BOOK OF DURHAM CITY

West view of the Cathedral with the Fulling Mill on the river banks from
slightly upstream, 1843.

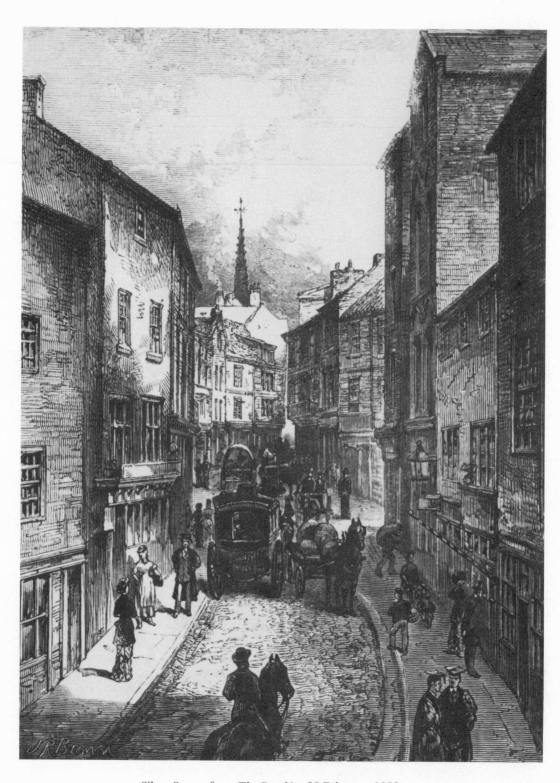

Silver Street, from *The Graphic* of 2 February 1883.

THE BOOK OF DURHAM CITY

BY

PETER CLACK BA MLitt FSA(Scot)

BARRACUDA BOOKS LIMITED
BUCKINGHAM, ENGLAND
MCMLXXXV

PUBLISHED BY BARRACUDA BOOKS LIMITED
BUCKINGHAM, ENGLAND
AND PRINTED BY
BURGESS & SONS (ABINGDON) LIMITED
ABINGDON, ENGLAND

BOUND BY
J.W. BRAITHWAITE & SON LIMITED
WOLVERHAMPTON, ENGLAND

JACKET PRINTED BY
CHENEY & SONS LIMITED
BANBURY, OXON

PHOTOLITHOGRAPHY BY
SOUTH MIDLANDS LITHOPLATES LIMITED
LUTON, ENGLAND

DISPLAY SET IN BASKERVILLE
AND TEXT SET IN 10½/12pt BASKERVILLE BY
KEY COMPOSITION
NORTHAMPTON, ENGLAND

ISBN 0 86023 202 6

Contents

Acknowledgements

Much of the material on which this book is based has been collected piecemeal since 1974, when I started to work in Durham. Excavation and watching briefs that I have carried out in Durham City since 1975 have been funded by the Department of the Environment and latterly English Heritage (Historic Buildings and Monuments Commission (England)). Excavations carried out before 1978 were partly funded by the Manpower Services Commission. The collection of a great deal of the documentary material was also funded by the Manpower Services Commission. At Beaurepaire an extended excavation programme has been jointly funded by Durham City and County Councils and Durham University.

In the course of collecting material for this book I have been most courteously assisted by the staffs of the Dean and Chapter Library, Durham Cathedral, the Department of Palaeography and Diplomatic of the University of Durham (in both its divisions), Durham University Library, Durham City Library, the Reading Room and Local Information Room, Department of Archaeology, Durham University, Durham County Record Office, and Newcastle upon Tyne Central Library. In addition, I have made use of the Blackgate Library of the Society of Antiquaries of Newcastle upon Tyne, Newcastle University Library and the J. D. Cowen Library of the Department of Archaeology in Newcastle University.

So many people have helped me to understand Durham since 1974 that to name them all is impossible. A select few are: Miss E. L. Addis, Mr M. Anderson, Mr R. Briggs, Messrs Burt, Hart and Pratt, Solicitors, Mr A. Clark, Prof R. J. Cramp, Mrs J. Crosby, Mr R. Dewar, Dr B. Dobson, Mrs J. L. Drury, Mr A. G. Esslemont, Hon Secretary, United Reformed Church History Society, Mr J. H. Fox, Hon Secretary, Durham Chamber of Trade, Mr B. H. Gill, Mr J. Gosden, Mr P. F. Gosling, Miss R. B. Harbottle, Dr and Mrs J. Hawgood, Mrs G. N. Ivy, Mr D. Jones, Mr I. MacIntyre, Mr J. MacKay, Mr T. Middlemass, Mrs P. Lee, Mr P. Mussett, Mr R. C. Norris, Mr C. F. O'Brien, Mr and Mrs C. Redpath, Dr B. K. Roberts, Mr H. M. Roberts, Mr M. Snape, Miss H. Threadgill, Mr N. Till, Mr E. Walton, and Mr D. Wilcock. It is a matter of much sadness that four people who helped me a great deal will never see this book: Wilfred Dodds, Eleanor Heppell, Eric Parsons and Kenneth Pattinson.

To the many people who have commented on ideas thrown out during evening classes, who have stood on the side of an excavation or who have come up after a Guided Walk and said 'I remember . . .', I offer my best thanks.

Tom Middlemass and Trevor Woods have done nearly all the photographic work involved in preparing the illustrations. I am grateful to Durham City Council, Durham County Record Office, the Dean and Chapter Library, Durham Cathedral, Department of Palaeographic and Diplomatic (Prior's Kitchen), Durham University Library, Professor R. J. Cramp, Department of Archaeology, Durham University, the Freemen and Guilds of Durham City, Mr A. H. Reed, Mr and Mrs J. M. Balfour, J. & G. Archibald Ltd, Hugh MacKay Ltd, Julian Bennett, Mr A. R. Middleton, Archaeological Unit for North-East England, Mr A. Clark, Secretary, Durham Regatta, and Mr J. L. Myers for permission to reproduce items in their care. In one or two cases I have failed to trace a copyright holder or to establish whether an item is in copyright. If I have erred, I can only apologise.

Eric Cambridge has read and commented on a draft of part of the book and Geoffrey Milburn has read part of the chapter on Churches in an earlier form. My wife has read the entire text and has made many useful comments.

All those who have assisted with the essential subscription facility are gratefully acknowledged. Finally, it is pleasing to thank David Gerard for conceiving and writing *A Prospect of Durham* specially for this book — making an unique contribution to our appreciation of the influence of the past upon the present, and of the present upon the future.

Foreword

by the Right Worshipful the Mayor of Durham, Councillor A. Crooks JP

It is with much pleasure and anticipated deep interest that I commend this *Book of Durham City*.

Peter Clack has researched and literally unearthed many exciting, stimulating and little known facts and evidence which have influenced the appearance and structure of our magnificent City.

I am particularly interested in the chapter dealing with buildings, as I have lived all my life within sight of the Prior's country house at Beaurepaire, and of course the buildings in the City and the market place have gone much unnoticed, despite their remarkable architectural features and historical significance.

The chapter on trade and industry will be of particular interest to the freemen of the various guilds of the City, who still meet regularly in the Guildhall.

The details of the origins and development of individual firms and local industries will be of interest to all who live and work in Durham. I am delighted to be given this opportunity to thank Peter Clack for this fascinating and impressive account of Durham City.

Durham City from near St Giles' church in 1834.

West view of the Cathedral with the Fulling Mill on the river banks from
slightly upstream, 1843. (Durham Advertiser)

Introduction

To write a dry-as-dust history of Durham that, like John Henderson, speaks like a ledger, is to do a disservice both to the City and to the reader. To pretend to provide a definitive account of Durham's history in the short compass of this book is equally a disservice.

What I have attempted to do is provide an impression, painted with a broad brush, of Durham's changing past, that combines the evidence from excavations, standing buildings both great and small and the incredibly rich documentary sources. It is the nature of accounts such as this that they betray bias on the part of the author. This I have tried to overcome, but in the end only the reader can tell whether I have been successful in my description of this incomparable City. For those who wish to know in more detail my sources of information, a fully referenced copy of this book will be lodged with Durham City Library.

Dedication

To Heather, Daniel, Sam and Toby.

A Prospect of Durham

Here the struck hour
Rims the cultured day,
Eleison of leaves,
The marching songs of roots
Veil the swift Wear.

In the morning of the ravens
Over the place of silence
A currency of love
Begot the town,
Circuit of power
Where the river ran;
The black sky must have seemed
Shot through with gold
Above the tumulus
Ten centuries raised
In stone-faced majesty.

Aloof, the centuries conspire
To hold us
In lettered psalter, purple stole,
Cloister and crozier
Within grey walls.
But younger shapes on older shadows fell
Across the eight-bridged city
When black earth
Under the gated sepulchre
Shook from millenial seams
Colliers and co-eds
To bruise the Saint's demesne,
Cunning of new coinage.

Old outcrop, time's capsule,
In plain processional of kingdom come
Move upon the waters,
Under the sun's sharp spears revolve.
Now heal, now hold
A new communion
Where the Swan's road runs
Yesterday, today and then today.

David Gerard

South east view of the Cathedral from Elvet Banks in 1843.

ABOVE: The South West Prospect of the City of Durham by Samuel and Nathaniel Buck, 1745. BELOW: Prebend's Bridge and the Cathedral, 1787.

Viewed From Afar

Surrounded by hills, and on a hill itself, stands the heart of Durham City, defended on three sides by a gorge cut deep into the Coal Measures by the River Wear. The Pennine foothills lie no great distance to the west, while the sharply rising Magnesian Limestone Escarpment, some three miles east of Durham, marks the western limit of the East Durham Plateau which dips gently towards the North Sea.

In 1626 Robert Hegge, a native of Durham, included the following description of his birthplace in his *Legend of St Cuthbert*:

'This reverend aged Abby is seated in the heart of the City, advanced upon the Shoulders of an high Hill and encompassed againe with the higher Hills, that he that hath seene the situation of this Citty, hath seene the Map of Sion, and may save a journey to the Jerusalem. She is girded almost rown'd with the renown'd River of *Weer* in which, as in a Glasse of Crystall, shee might once have beheld the beauty, but now the ruine of her walls . . .'

This partisan description should be balanced by that of John Ray, the late 17th century natural historian. Durham to him was simply 'a large scattering town, but in most men's account pleasantly situate'.

In the form that we now know Durham, it consists of several rather scattered parts which have separate origins in the early history of the town. Old Elvet, New Elvet, Gilesgate, Crossgate and Framwellgate form the suburbs of Durham City proper, which nestles under the protecting cliffs of the Castle on the narrowest part of the long ridge leading up to Gilesgate. It is as well to start by viewing the City and suburbs as a whole before exploring their several origins and histories. Allom and Rose in 1832 said of Durham City and its environs that 'from what point so ever they may be surveyed, [they] present an unique and striking appearance'.

William Hutchinson first drew attention to the picturesque nature of Durham's situation and presented several views of the City and its monuments. Perhaps the finest of his descriptions — indeed, perhaps the finest ever written of Durham — is that looking south from St Giles' churchyard, which scarcely needs an illustration to accompany it. Unfortunately the view is now obscured by trees growing on the south side of the churchyard.

Others both before and since have added to the magnificent series of views of the peninsula set within its bowl. The prospect from Observatory Hill, illustrated by Samuel and Nathaniel Buck in 1745 and poorly copied for Hutchinson's *History* shows the 'hanging gardens' of the South Bailey as well as the whole of the suburbs. This is almost the only place from which to illustrate the topography of Durham in one drawing. There have been many changes since 1745, not only to individual structures, but also to the town. The town has grown in all directions since 1800, and especially since 1900. The alterations and additions bear a greater or lesser degree of merit in the eye of the beholder, filtered as they are by the aesthetic prejudices of the era to which he or she belongs. However, from whichever angle one views

Durham, the Cathedral is the dominant feature, more especially so on a dark and dismal day, when a shaft of light pierces the clouds to fix upon it. These are not infrequent moments, when St Cuthbert still seems to be taking an interest in his resting place, despite scientific disturbances.

ABOVE: West view of the Cathedral with the Fulling Mill on the river banks, 1846. BELOW: Castle and Framwellgate Bridge in 1824 by Joseph Bouet. (DC Add MS 95)

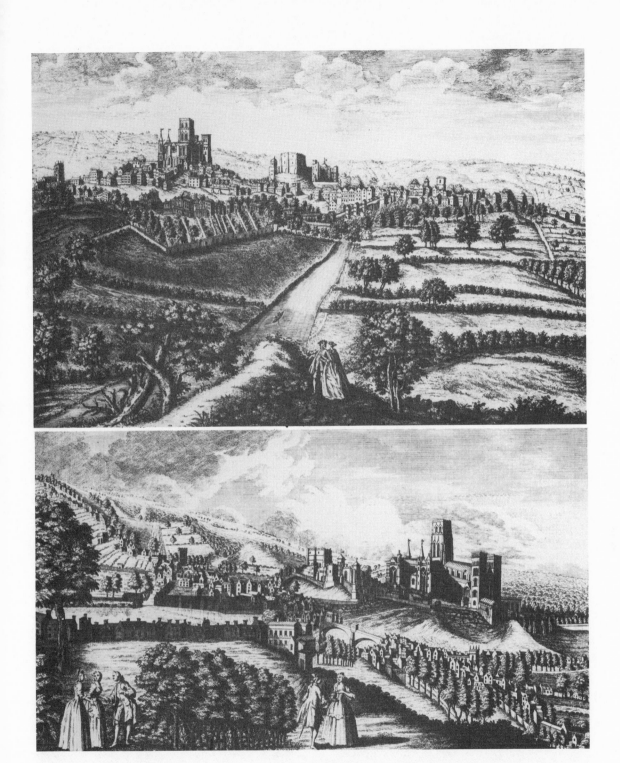

ABOVE: An East view of Durham from Pelaw Wood hill (*ie* below St Giles) by T. Forster, 1754. (DC) BELOW: Durham City from above Framwellgate by T. Forster, 1754. (DC)

ABOVE: Durham City from Castle Chare by Maria Pixell, 1782;
BELOW: from the top of the North Road by R. W. Billings in 1843.

ABOVE: Cathedral and Castle from the North Road in 1846 and with
BELOW: Framwellgate, from the railway viaduct in about 1956. (DC)

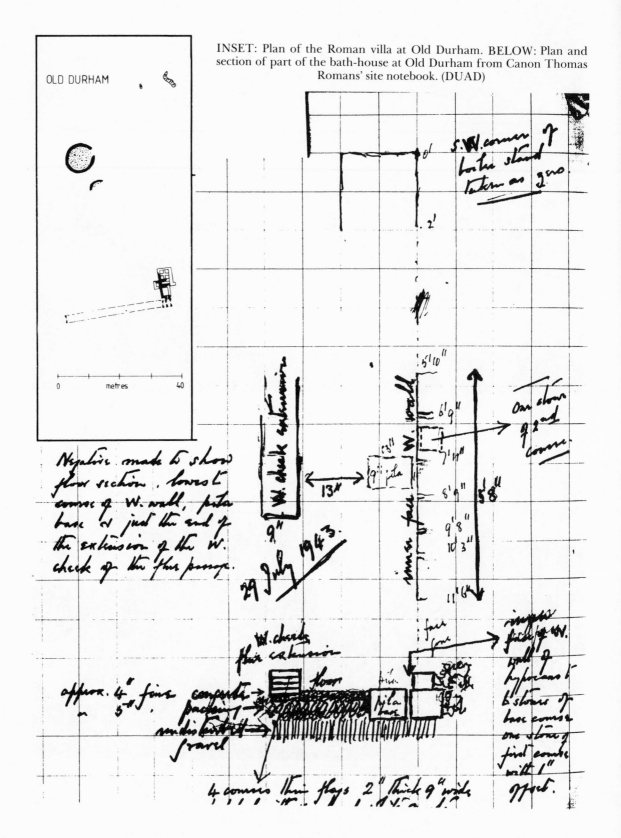

INSET: Plan of the Roman villa at Old Durham. BELOW: Plan and section of part of the bath-house at Old Durham from Canon Thomas Romans' site notebook. (DUAD)

St Cuthbert's Landfall

Below Gilesgate and east of Pelaw Woods is the manor and farm of Old Durham, in the grounds of which a Roman villa was found in 1940. In the course of the ensuing decade various people, chief among them the Master of Sherburn Hospital, Canon Thomas Romans, excavated and recorded the remains as they came to light in front of a steadily advancing quarry face. The villa started life as a pre-Roman native farmstead which was later 'romanised', to become a villa occupied in the second and fourth centuries. Like other villas in the north-east, it seems to have been abandoned in the third century, but this may be a factor of destruction without record rather than one of occupation history.

In more recent years, some Roman material has come to light in the Cathedral precincts. Excavations which took place in the west range undercroft, before its conversion to the present Treasury in 1977, revealed some medieval paving, beneath which was a coin of Vespasian and a few sherds of pottery. In 1983 and in 1985 a few more sherds of Roman pottery were found elsewhere in the precincts. As one swallow does not make a summer, so these few scraps of evidence for occupation in the Roman period on the peninsula do not make a Roman fort. More likely, they suggest the presence of a native farmstead occupied then.

Two Roman roads point towards Durham, but neither reaches it. The western is a branch of Dere Street, which comes off that road at Willington but fails to reach Durham. The eastern is a road that starts at the Tees by Middleton St George but, where it is supposed to run at Coxhoe, excavation has revealed no trace. The most likely route for a Roman road at Durham would be to pass along the top of the hills that formed Elvet and Framwellgate Moors until colonised by Durham's industrial housing.

Once out of the Roman period there is no firm evidence for any settlements in the area until AD 763, in which year, according to the *Anglo-Saxon Chronicle*, Peohtwine was consecrated Bishop of Whithorn at Elvet on 17 July. By Elvet is meant the area in the vicinity of St Oswald's Church, for what is now called Old Elvet was not created until the twelfth century. The consecration suggests that Elvet was then a far more important place than now. There was almost certainly a church there, probably built in timber, for the consecration of the Bishop. All traces of that church have now disappeared. By that date too, there might have been a small village of farmers and their families gathered round the church like pilgrims at a shrine. It is possible that the slightly unusual dedication of the church to St Oswald may reflect a tradition (now lost) of that saint having visited the area before his death in 642.

Elvet will not have been the only village in the immediate area in the eighth century. Several villages around Durham were named for the first time in the seventh or eighth centuries, since their names reflect purely topographic features (*eg*: Shadforth: shallow ford; Cassop: valley of the cats; Sherburn: bright burn; Shincliffe: cliff of ghosts).

The vision that we must carry in our minds when considering the arrival of St Cuthbert's community in AD 995 is not one of desolation, nor that of Robert Hegge, who described the peninsula as 'more beholding to Nature for Fortification than Fertilitie; where thick Wood both hindred the Stones from viewing the Earth, and the Earth from the prospect of Heaven'. Rather is it of a number of small, probably muddy villages near the peninsula, with their fields tilled by slow-moving oxen. The Durham peninsula might have been well-mantled in trees, but there may also have been some cultivation or at least exploitation of that wood for fires, house-building, grazing for cattle, pigs etc. At that time woodland was too precious a resource to waste. The earlier Roman occupation on the top of the peninsula will have caused the woodland there to be cleared and this clearing might well have been maintained by the inhabitants of Elvet.

This is the general context in which we must view the establishment of St Cuthbert's community on the peninsula. Symeon of Durham tells how in AD 883 the community fled Lindisfarne in the face of Viking raiders, and settled at Chester-le-Street. In 995 the threat of further Scandinavian troubles was sufficient for the community of St Cuthbert to collect all its belongings, livestock and holy relics, including St Cuthbert, and move south to the safety of Ripon. There they remained for four months until King Ethelred bought peace. Intending, so we are told, to return to Chester-le-Street, they came north. On reaching a hill called *Wrdelau*, the carriage or cart on which St Cuthbert's coffin was placed became immoveable. They fasted and prayed to learn the cause. After a time the Divine will was revealed to Eadmer, one of the community, that they were to proceed to Dunhelme and there provide a new home for St Cuthbert. Later legend has it that they had no idea where this place was until, after casting round east Durham for a time, they heard a woman ask another where her cow was and received the reply that it was on Dunholme. The community then followed her to the fastness, which was well wooded apart from a clearing on top. The story of St Cuthbert's coffin becoming immoveable is a grace-note added to a plain tale. The Dun Cow legend is a further addition. When in Chester-le-Street, they must have known of Durham as a place so strongly defended by nature that man's hand was needed to carry out only slight works to make it thoroughly defensible against any adversary.

In the first instance the community built a covering of boughs for St Cuthbert's coffin, until they were able to build a more permanent church in timber. The temporary resting place may have been in or about St Oswald's Church, from which place has come a large cross shaft. Once the community had built a suitable church to house St Cuthbert, his coffin was moved up the hill with all due ceremony and installed in its new resting place. This temporary church, known as the White Church, probably because it was of whitewashed timber, remained for three years, while Bishop Aldhun built a stone church, using labour impressed from the Tees to the Coquet by his son-in-law Uhtred, Earl of Northumbria. As Martin Carver has noted, this was 'a commitment which indicates that the development of the Durham site was scarcely the devotional exercise of a beleaguered convent, but a central political event'. This stone church stood until the present one was begun in 1093, and probably for some years after, protecting St Cuthbert until the translation to his present location in the shrine east of the high altar in 1104.

ABOVE: Enclosure ditch and remains of the bath house at Old Durham. (DUAD) BELOW: Part of Symeon of Durham's account of AD 995 in *Historia Dunelmensis Ecclesia*. (DUL, Cosin MS V.II.6,f51r)

...actu pbabilis monachus; Cui pbitatis lau
dem a maiorib; sibi tradita indigene pene
ons ac si eu hodie uident. predicare solent.
Anno autē ab incarnatione dni nongente
simo nonagesimo qnto. impii u regis
Ethelredi septimo decimo. idem antistes
incipiente ia accepti prefulatᵒ sexto anno.
celesti premonitus oraculo ut cū incorrupto
sissimi patris corpore quantocius fugiens

Lib. III. Cap. I.

23

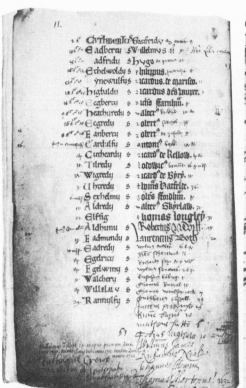

LEFT: List of the Bishops of Lindisfarne, Chester-le-Street and Durham, compiled by Symeon of Durham and brought up to date from time to time. (DUL Cosin MS V.II.6,f6v) BELOW: The Dun Cow statue as recorded by Hutchinson in 1787, and RIGHT: after 19th century restoration. (DC)

24

The First Town

The church and town of Durham were established by the secular community serving St Cuthbert. In 1083, however, Bishop William of St Calais removed the secular community and in its stead installed a regular Benedictine monastery, drawn partly from the establishments at Jarrow and Monkwearmouth. Until then the Bishop had been part of the community, itself dependent on revenues from lands granted by many different people. The separation of Bishop and community after 1083 meant separate residences and separate revenues, for the endowment was henceforth divided between the two.

The earlier community must have lived in a village of rectangular wooden houses in the shade of the grand and gleaming stone church. Village and church were the focus of a town that grew rapidly on the peninsula. The dead from community and perhaps also town were buried, each on a bed of charcoal, where later burials took place under the present chapter house, and possibly further east as well.

Probably, some residents originally came as impressed labour in the late 10th century, and stayed, while others joined them to live in the area immediately north of the church. When the Scots attacked Durham in 1040 they were unable to take the town. The same forced labour perhaps constructed defensive works on the most vulnerable part of the occupied area: the cliff top on the north side. These were probably earthen ramparts, now lost to view beneath the subsequent massive masonry of convent and all-embracing stone Castle. Not only was there a town within these defences in 1040, but the heads of slain Scots were displayed on poles in the market place. Within fifty years of its foundation, Durham had become a stoutly-defended centre of trade and industry.

There is some firm evidence for this early town for, beneath the ground to the rear of Nos 61-3 Saddler Street, excavations revealed the remains of wattle buildings, surrounded by middens containing leather offcuts and waste from shoe making and repairing, as well as domestic refuse. The earliest structures are broadly contemporary with the Church and were rebuilt several times before about 1200, when the main building moved to the front and faced onto Saddler Street. While the early houses were set well back in their plots, the black organic material from the middens ran right up to the present line of Saddler Street, though at least 3.5 metres deeper than today's ground level. As a result of this excavation we can safely say that the first town straggled at least half way down Saddler Street.

The earliest structures and occupation deposits under the houses on the south side of the Market Place, and at the bottom of Saddler Street, on the Castle side, are 12th century and later. Here there are no deep deposits below street level, but on the river side of Saddler Street they are considerable. The foundations of the rear extension of Carricks the Bakers, for example, cut waterlogged, smelly organic material at least twenty feet below street level. The houses on the east (river) side of Saddler Street all have at least one, if not two basement storeys to counteract the precipitous fall of the ground on that side. The same is true of buildings on the east and west sides of the Market Place as well as the north side of Silver Street.

When these observations are joined with others made over a number of years, and the depth of 'made ground' is stripped away from Durham's present topography, its original form, and the constraints that determined it, begin to emerge. The Market Place and lower part of Saddler Street were probably at or about their present level. Saddler Street had a precipice dropping down to the river on one side and a narrow, flattish area curtailed by a cliff rising under the Castle on the other side. While the original upper Saddler Street may have sloped, the old ground surface of the middle street was about 3.5 metres below present level. Today's steep incline at the junction of Saddler Street, Owengate and North Bailey is caused largely by the subterannean remains of the massive North Gate, which still survives one storey down at No 46. All the way along the North Bailey the steet level has risen at least 2 to 2.5 metres but here, the flat area, narrow at the bottom of Saddler Street, has widened out considerably. While the precipice to the river still survives, on the west side the diminishing cliff is obscured by houses. Those on the east side of Palace Green are built on top of it, while those on the west side of North Bailey occupy its foot.

Further south, there is less evidence: at Bow Lane the ground fell away steeply from the South Bailey to the river. The old ground surface is about 2.5 metres below the present street, though the Cathedral to the west retains its original level. South of these, there has been some accumulation of soil. On the north side of South Bailey near St Mary-the-Less, it approaches 3-4 metres, though only about 2.5 metres in the roadway. The western side of the peninsula must always have been a cliff, which both Convent and Castle used to their advantage. The steepness of the slope on that side of the peninsula is apparent in the western half of Moatside Lane as it descends to Framwellgate Bridge. The old ground surface is probably 2.5 to 3 metres below Silver Street and is considerably deeper under Moatside Lane, on the Castle side of which there is a great depth of rubbish thrown out from the Castle (2 metres of 18th and 19th century material alone in one place!). The Castle was clearly built on a cliff whose slope has softened with the discharge of rubbish.

When the community first came to Durham, there will have been the long sloping ridge running down from the area of St Giles, with a steadily narrowing crest as it descended to its narrowest point near the later St Nicholas church. From there to the great cliff, almost cutting off the peninsula, it widened and levelled out. The steep sides leading down to the river on either side merged with the cliffs which protected the south, east and west sides of the topmost area. There was probably a narrow rising ledge on the east side (later to become Saddler Street), the sole access, which widened as it reached the top. A gentle slope from the southern cliffs rose to the high point of the plateau under the later Priory. The ground was more or less level from there to the northern cliff and it was this small, level area of ground that held the first Convent, town and defensive earthworks.

ABOVE: Symeon of Durham's account of the appointment of Bishop William of St Calais in *Historia Dunelmensis Ecclesia*. (DUL, Cosin MS V.II.6,f77v) BELOW: Plan of Durham as it might have been before AD 1100.

153.

ib. IV.
Cap. I.

TRANSACTIS
post occisioné walcheri epi sex
mensib; & decé diebus: anno im
pii willi qnto decimo abbas mo
nasterij sci martyris yincentij
WILLELMUS ab ipso rege elect. epatú dunhel
mensis ecclé qnta idus nouébris suscepit regen
dú. ordinatio ú illi aliquanto p idest tertia
nonas ianuarii. uidelicet inoctauis sci iohis
euangelistę die diica presente rege & epis
totu anglię astantib; ab archiepo eboracensi
Thoma solenniti est adimpleta. Hic quidem

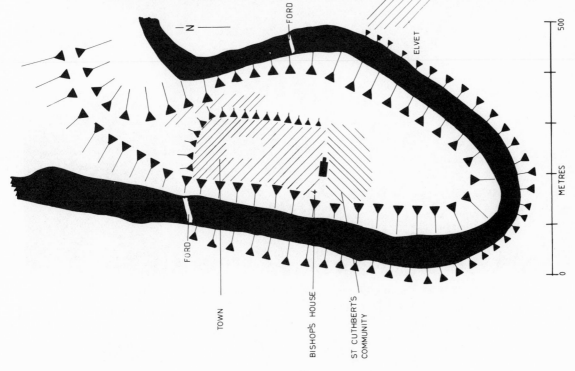

LEFT: Early medieval structures, 61-63 Saddler Street. (MOHC).
RIGHT: Stamford Ware cresset lamp from 79 Saddler Street. (TM)
CENTRE: Ground behind Silver Street sloping down towards the river.
(PAGC) BELOW: Durham City below the naturally defended plateau of
the peninsula. (TM)

28

Promise of Heaven

'Most Cathedrals are in the last analysis only buildings:
Durham is an invention' — E. J. Burrow *Guide to Durham*, 1920.

There is a crack through which, if we peer closely, we may appreciate the glory of Durham's past. Today we have but a few splashes of paint in the Cathedral where once there was an abundance, and few of the interior fittings have survived. We can see from the west end of the nave to the east end of the choir where, before the Reformation, that view would have been interrupted by a screen across the east end of the nave, as well as the choir screen surmounted by an organ.

To have gone from ill-paved streets and poorly-lit small houses into the huge space, trapped in stone, resonant with plainsong and organ, lit in glittering colours from the windows, the brilliantly painted and gilded Priory Church must have epitomised the promise of heaven to the pre-Reformation townspeople. This vision is in sharp contrast to both its humble origins as a whitewashed timber church, replaced in 998 by a stone church and the rather plain if imposing structure of today.

While the group of buildings ranged round the cloister's four sides had been started in the 1070s, they were only completed shortly before 1300. In the subsequent 240 years they were constantly altered and repaired. Before 1300 major works were separately carried out on the church and the claustral buildings. The present Cathedral building — the conventual church — was begun in 1093, some ten years after the secular clergy had been removed. Before then, conventual buildings for the monks and their various offices had been partly built.

Walcher, Bishop from 1071 until his murder in 1080, started to build the east range, of which only a tiny fragment still survives, encapsulated in later work. His chapter house (if ever built) is now gone, but the prison immediately south of the chapter house still survives, under the abandoned day stair from the first monastic dormitory. This work was completed by the succeeding Bishop, William of St Calais (1081-1091) who also built the refectory undercroft on the south range. These buildings will have been planned in relation to the great stone church completed in 998, which a recent survey has shown probably lay entirely south of the present Cathedral church. This first cloister was also a little smaller than the present one.

The church itself was started in 1093, building from east to west. The choir vault was completed by 29 August 1104, when St Cuthbert was translated from the older church to his new resting place within the eastern apse. The nave walls were completed by 1128 and the vaults five years later. The Chapter House was then either built or rebuilt between 1133 and 1141 and, in the time of Bishop William of St Barbe (1144-52), the monastic dormitory was possibly moved to its present location in the west range.

Bishop Hugh of le Puiset (1154-95) made his mark by erecting an extension, perhaps an aisle around the apse. This was never completed either because it started to crack or because of monastic opposition. The incomplete aisle was then dismantled, and the materials — including columns of specially imported Purbeck marble — were re-used in the 1170s, in the construction of the western Galilee. This five-aisled building probably had three central aisles under one roof, and the north and south aisles under a series of transverse roofs. While its original purpose is uncertain, it may be consistent with the later functions of housing a Lady Chapel, ecclesiastical court and serving as an assembly point for processions on Sundays and Feast days. The closing years of the twelfth and opening years of the thirteenth centuries saw the building of both the Prior's lodging, probably under the present Deanery, and the western towers.

If the Galilee was the great addition of the twelfth century, then the Chapel of the Nine Altars was its counterpart in the thirteenth. Fund raising for the chapel, built as an eastern transept to the church, started in 1253, when the stone vault over the choir was full of fissures and cracks and liable to disintegrate. Work began in 1242 and had reached about half way by 1253, for in June of that year a new high altar to St Mary the Virgin and the central five of the nine altars in the east transept were consecrated. The southern limb of the transept was completed in 1274, when the two southernmost altars were consecrated. The completion of the northern limb was perhaps before 1274, perhaps shortly after 1279, which is the last date for which there is evidence for fund raising for this transept.

At the same time that work on the Nine Altars was proceeding, the claustral buildings were being extended. Prior Bertram of Middleton (1244-58) added the chapel of St Nicholas to the Prior's Lodging. The great tower (not that which we see today) was built between 1258 and 1290 and a vestry on the south side of the choir was added in the 1290s.

The completion of the Convent and its church concided with the eruption of a dispute about conventual independence and bishop's rights. It had flared up earlier in the thirteenth century, but had been settled by an agreement known as 'le Convenit' between Prior and Convent on the one hand, and Bishop Richard Poor on the other. This time Bishop Antony Bek (1283-1310) and Prior Richard of Hoton (1289-1308) were more obstinate and half Europe echoed with their wrangling. It started in 1300 when Bek exerted his rights of Visitation over the monastery, insisting on a small retinue, the Priory objecting to its size. Bek resorted to brute force, blockading the convent from 23 May to late September 1300 with only two intermissions, stopping food supplies and messages. In early August he cut off the the Priory's water and broke its mill on the banks of the Wear. After numerous appeals to the Archbishop of York, the King of Rome and vast expense, the dispute was resolved in 1310.

In the fourteenth century, and in particular during the priorate of John Fossour (1341-74), there was much renovation and improvement. The remarkable octagonal kitchen on the south range was built under the direction of John Lewyn, best known for his work on northern castles. The stupendous altar screen of Caen stone, erected largely at the expense of John, Lord Neville, was also constructed. It was made in London, shipped to Newcastle and then taken by road to Durham. The whole process took between four and eight years, completed in 1380, when a new high altar was consecrated against the west face of the screen. A year later, Bishop Thomas Hatfield (1345-1381) died and was buried in his tomb under the throne he had erected after 1373 on the south side of the choir.

In the late fourteenth century the roof of the dormitory in the west range became seriously defective. The upper part was dismantled and rebuilt by the end of October 1404. Bishop Skirlaw (1388-1405) largely financed the work and prepared his own tomb and chantry chapel in the north aisle of the choir, completed by 1403.

There was a series of improvements during the fifteenth century. The cloister was entirely rebuilt in the first two decades, apart from the glazing, the cost borne jointly by Bishop

Skirlaw's executors and Bishop Langley (1406-37). Prior Wessington (1416-1446) built a library on the first floor between the south transept and the chapter house. Other works carried out in his time included rebuilding the Infirmary (1419-1430), erecting a new laver in the cloister opposite the frater door (1432), renovating the Prior's lodging (1424-36) and extensive repairs to the monastic guest house. Wessington is also said to have built the Sacrist's Exchequer on the north side of the choir.

There were two other principal works. Bishop Langley (1406-37) restored the Galilee (1429-35), altering the roof structure, inserting new windows and adding the massive western buttresses. Contrary to tradition he did not add the freestone columns in each of the piers supporting the arcades. They were part of the original design of the Galilee. He built his tomb and chantry chapel before the altar of the Virgin, placed before the original great west door of the nave.

On 27 May 1429 the central tower was struck by lightning and set on fire. It was repaired over the next eight years but by 1456 was threatening to fall. The Prior and Convent appealed to the Bishop for help and advice but in 1459 the tower was again struck by lightning, this time totally destroyed and the church roof badly burnt. The necessary repairs lasted from the mid-1460s to at least the late 1480s, probably without a break.

The last important piece of building work before the Dissolution was the rebuilding of the Abbey Gateway, with the Chapel of St Helen above, by Prior Richard Castell (1494-1519).

ABOVE: North facade of the Cathedral drawn by George Nicholson in 1780 before any restoration, and BELOW: in 1956. Note the addition of spires to the corner towers of the Chapel of Nine Altars and pinnacles to the western towers. The porch to the North doorway has also been altered. (DC)

31

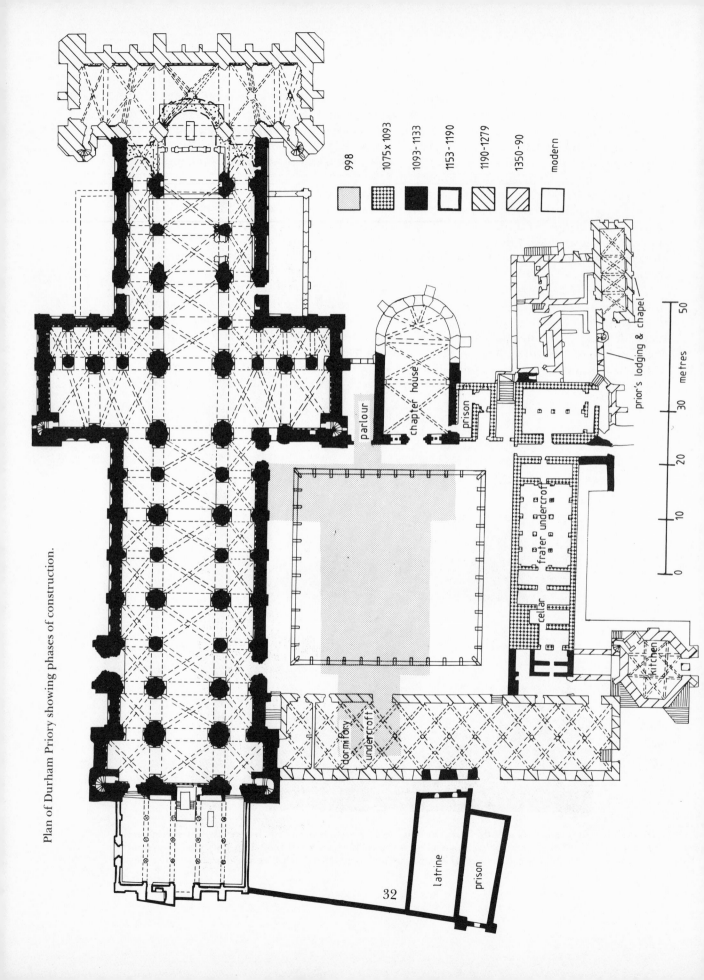

Plan of Durham Priory showing phases of construction.

998
1075 x 1093
1093 - 1133
1153 - 1190
1190 - 1279
1350 - 90
modern

prior's lodging & chapel

parlour

chapter house

prison

cellar

frater undercroft

kitchen

dormitory
undercroft

latrine

prison

32

metres

50
30
20
10
0

LEFT: The nave looking east, showing the 17th century choir screen,
and RIGHT: the choir looking west from the high altar both in 1843, R.
W. Billings. BELOW: The east end of the Galilee showing the place of
the altars of the Holy Cross (N), Blessed Virgin Mary and Cardinal
Langley's tomb (centre) and the Venerable Bede (S).

Copy of the letter written by Prior John Wessington to Bishop Langley when lightning struck the tower in 1429. (DPAD: PK: Reg II parv, f39) 'Most reverend and my most singular Lord. Because, I doubt not, there has reached your ears an account of the misfortune which has lately happened to the belfry of your Church of Durham, to console in some part your grief, I lay before you in this my letter, a correct statement of the fact. During the night before the day of Corpus Christi, from ten o'clock until two in the morning, there were in these our parts thunderings and lightnings dreadful, and such as were never before heard; and especially a short time before one o'clock, such was the violence of the thunder during the time we were at matins that we believed a great part of the Church had fallen. At which time, as is most probable, the upper part of the great belfry under the dome called in English 'the Poll' was struck with lightning, but the fire did not manifest itself till seven o'clock in the following morning — from which hour until twelve the fire continued burning dreadfully, and the dome being of copper or brass, and containing in circumference two ells and three quarters, being most intensely heated, fell down upon the Church, dragging with it its heavy iron work and burning timber, but the place of its fall was one calculated to receive no great harm. Blessed be the Most High — in this fact God acted graciously. For the ten or twelve men who were toiling to extinguish the fire, although surrounded by burning wood, drenched with molten lead and struck by pieces of blazing timber, yet remained unhurt: and so through the prayers of the people, who had assembled in very great numbers, by the will of God the fire was totally extinguished soon after mid-day. Whereupon the hymn, called *Te Deum Laudamus* was most devoutly sung by us and the multitude of people, because there was no one who witnessed the conflagration, who does not consider it a miracle that the whole belfry, and in consequence the Church, with its adjacent buildings did not fall a prey to so devouring a fire. That portion of the upper part of the belfry which has been destroyed by the fire, is estimated to be twenty feet in length. May the Highest preserve your most reverend Lordship in prosperity to a good old age.' Written at Durham 27 May 1429. Translation by James Raine.

ABOVE LEFT: The Norman doorway on the south side of the nave, by Joseph Bouet, 1824. (DC Add Ms 95) RIGHT: The east end of the Chapter House as drawn by John Carter in 1795 and demolished in 1799. BELOW LEFT: Lantern in the roof of the Prior's kitchen drawn by R. W. Billings in 1843. RIGHT: The Abbey Gate with St Katherine's chapel above, by Joseph Bouet in 1824. (DC Add MS 95)

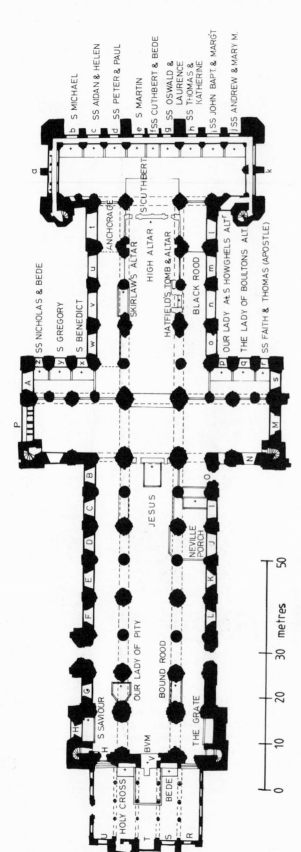

Plan of the Cathedral showing the location and dedication of altars and the principal saints depicted in the windows as they were recorded in the late 16th century: a: Joseph's window; b: Eight Orders of Angels; c: Saints Aidan, Helen, Blessed Virgin Mary and Archangel Gabriel; d: Saints Peter, Paul, Cuthbert, Aidan and Ceadda; e: Saints Martin and Edmund; f: Saints Cuthbert, Bede and Oswald; g: Saints Oswald, Laurence and Cuthbert; h: Saint Katherine and the Blessed Virgin Mary; i: Saint John the Baptist and Saint Margeret; j: Saints Andrew, Mary Magdalene and the Four Doctors of the Church; k: Saint Cuthbert's window; l: Saints Cuthbert, Oswald, George and the Blessed Virgin Mary; m: Saints Peter Andrew, James and John the Evangelist; n: Saints Thomas, James, Philip, and Bartholomew; o: Saints Barbara, Andrew, John the Evangelist, James, John the Baptist and the Blessed Virgin Mary; p: Saints Katherine, Margaret, Christopher, and John the Baptist; q: Saints John the Evangelist, Nicholas, Our Lady of Bolton, Stephen and John the Baptist; r: Blessed Virgin Mary, Saints Thomas, Leonard, Laurence and Bede; s: Crucifixion, St John the Evangelist; t: Saints Anne, Mary Magdalene, Mary Cleophe, Salome and the Blessed Virgin Mary; u: Saints Michael the Archangel, Katherine, Cuthbert and the Blessed Virgin Mary; v: Saints Oswald, Cuthbert and Gregory; w: Saints Aidan, Cuthbert, Mary and Oswald; x: Saints Gregory, and Ambrose; z: Saints Giles and Nicholas; A: Saints John the Baptist, the Blessed Virgin Mary and John the Evangelist; B: Crucifixion, the Blessed Virgin Mary and John the Evangelist; C: —; D: Saints Katherine, Oswald, Cuthbert, Bede and Edmund; E: —; F: —; G: Saints Oswald, Paul, Peter, and James. H: The Blessed Virgin Mary; I: Saints George, Oswald, the Blessed Virgin Mary, Christopher; J: God the Father and Son; Saint Cuthbert; K: the Blessed Virgin Mary; M: Te Deum window; N: the Blessed Virgin Mary, Saints Cuthbert, John the Baptist and the Evangelist and Anne; L: Archangel Gabriel, Blessed Virgin Mary; L: Saints Cuthbert, John the Baptist, Paul, John the Evangelist and Anne; L: Archangel Gabriel, Blessed Virgin Mary; M: Te Deum window; N: the Blessed Virgin Mary, Saints Cuthbert, John the Baptist and Oswald; O: Saints Oswald, Cuthbert and the Blessed Virgin Mary; P: The Four Doctors (of the church); R: Three Kings, Nativity, God Almighty, Holy Ghost; S: Saints Cuthbert, Bede, Aidan, Aldhun, Edmund, Eata, Nativity and the wedding in Galilee; T: the Blessed Virgin Mary, Saints Oswald, Wilfrid, Cedda, King Henry VI, Flight into Egypt; U: Kings Ailred, Guthred and Alfred, Saints Eadfrid and Ethelwold; Christ's Crucifixion and resurrection; V: The Tree of Jesse. Bishop Langley contributed windows f, g, O, T; Bishop Skirlaw, windows e, G, H; the Lords Neville, windows J, K, L; George Cornforth, window u; sub-prior William Seaton, window y.

36

Sermons in Glass

'. . . there remains that which is solemn and sublime, that which arises awes and yet elevates, that which by its durable grandeur shews the observer at once the power and the littleness of his own kind. And if perchance the traveller enters when the choral service, for which Durham is so justly famed to the ends of the kingdom, is being celebrated, and listens to the sonorous Amens of the unaccompanied choir, or hears in the anthem the organ rolling its sounds over roof and floor, till the whole vast edifice seems inundated with the musical waves and echoes back the tribute of praise, he will fairly confess that it is a combination of sight and sound with which few things of the kind can offer anything to compete, and that much of the true fame of Durham has its source within the walls of its Cathedral' — George Walker, *A Brief Sketch of Durham*, 1870.

This description of the Cathedral is as true today as it was in 1870. Earlier *The Rites of Durham* of the late 16th century, describes the Priory's church in all its glory before it was stripped of its multitude of ornaments.

The nine altars in the chapel of that name were ranged against the east wall, each covered with a richly decorated cloth, some with figures or paintings above. Separating each pair of altars was a wooden screen painted over 'with fine branches and flowers . . . most finely . . . pictured and gilded . . .' The walls, rising sheer to the stone vault above the altars, dwarfed everything else in the transept, even though the faces were broken by clustered columns of Frosterley marble which gently reflected the coloured light from the two tiers of windows. In the centre of the east wall was the large circular Catherine Window. It was reglazed at least twice before 1500, in about 1360 and 1410. Light from the north and south ends was transmitted by two large windows, that on the north being 'a goodly faire great glasse window . . . the which hath in yt all the whole storye of Joseph most artificially wrought in pictures in fine coloured glass according as it is sett forth in the bible verye good and godly to the beholders therof'. St Cuthbert's window on the south depicted his life.

The smaller windows were equally instructive, containing scenes from the lives of the saints above whose altars they were placed and painted in brilliant hues.

The chapel of the Nine Altars was separated from the choir and its aisles by St Cuthbert's shrine and the reredos to the high altar and by a screen below an anchorage at the east end of the north aisle. The anchorage, reached by steps which lay hard against St Cuthbert's shrine, had an altar on which was a 'marveillous faire roode with the most exquisite pictures of Marye and John'. On the south side of the high altar was the Black Rood of Scotland (won at the Battle of Neville's Cross in 1346) which had pictures of Christ flanked by St John and St Mary. These were all richly wrought in silver smoked black, each being three or four feet high and fixed to a wooden screen which reached the vault. The screen was decorated not only with 'curious painting' but was also painted red with a number of gold-covered lead stars set into it.

The south aisle of the choir was also decorated with four windows containing scenes from the lives of thirteen saints, as well as Christ's Nativity and Crucifixion. In the fourth light of the easternmost window appeared St George in armour (painted blue) slaying the dragon. The wall under the windows has intersecting blank arcades which were probably painted. The north side of the aisle contains Bishop Hatfield's tomb and effigy, brightly painted and gilded.

The four windows in the north wall of the north aisle had scenes from the lives of eleven saints. Bishop Skirlaw's tomb of marble sumptuously beset with brazen images, including that of the Bishop himself, was situated on the south side of the aisle. Over the west end of the aisle was a porch with an altar and rood painted with our Saviour 'the said Rood having marveilous sumptuous furniture for festivall dayes belonging to it'.

The choir, the heart of the daily ritual of the Convent, was the most richly decorated part of the church. The reredos was made in 1372-80 at the expense of John Lord Neville. It consists of a low wall with two doors on either side of the high altar leading to St Cuthbert's shrine with three tiers of canopied niches above, which once contained 107 statues. The three central niches over the high altar held the statues of St Mary, St Oswald and St Cuthbert, the three patron saints of the church. The whole was not in plain Caen stone as we see it today, but glittering in paint and gold.

At either end of the high altar was a gilt iron rail fixed in the screen, from each of which hung a white silk curtain or hanging. 'The dayly ornaments that were hunge both before the altar and a bove were of red velvet, wrought with great flowers of gold in imbroydered worke with many goodly pictures besides, beinge verye finely gilted, but the ornaments for the principall feast which was the assumption of our lady were all of white damaske all besett with pearle and pretious stones which made the ornaments more rich and gorgeous to behold'. Another pair of gilt iron rods supported a canopy over the high altar from which depended the golden, highly decorated pyx containing the sacrament. The pyx itself was protected by a white lawn cloth embroidered and decorated in gold and red silk. On the canopy was the silver figure of a pelican drawing blood from her breast to feed her young.

At Easter a great seven-branch candlestick known as the 'Paschall' stood before the high altar. It was supported by four dragon-shaped feet, each with one of the evangelists above, the surface of the whole being chased with figures of warriors on horseback. The central candlestick rose nearly forty feet in the air to support a square candle thirty feet high. This must indeed have been an awe-inspiring sight when lit with a new spark from a trap in the vault. When not in use the candlestick was dismantled and stored under the stairs leading up to the anchorage in the north aisle.

Before the high altar were three silver basins containing inner bronze basins to catch wax dripping from the candles that burned in them 'night and day, in token that the house was always watchinge to god'. There had been an organ or organs in the choir from at least 1264. In the 16th century there were three. That used every day, and known as the White Organ, was placed behind the wooden stalls at the west end of the choir on the south side. The organ opposite, 'The Cryers', was similarly placed behind the stalls and between the westernmost pillars on the north side. It was used only when the four Doctors of the church were read. On Principal or Feast Days a third organ, placed centrally above the choir door was used. The pipes were of fine wood and the doors that closed it were partly gilt inside and covered with branches and flowers on the outside with the name of Jesus 'gilted in gold . . . there was but 2 paire more of them in all England of the same makinge, one paire in Yorke and another in Paules'.

The choir door was set in a screen running the width of the choir which contained thirty-four coloured and gilded pictures or statues of kings, queens, godly founders and other benefactors, the counterpart to the book called the *Liber Vitae* on the High Altar. The principal organ was set into the east side of this screen over the door, while the pictures occupied the west side.

There were three bells in the tower above the junction of transepts, nave and choir which were rung by four men who slept in the church. The pair who slept in a small chamber immediately east of the Neville chantry chapel had charge of the copes, vestments, silver censers and everything to do with the high altar. The other pair, who slept in a chamber in the North Transept against the Sacrist's Exchequer, were responsible for sweeping and cleaning the church, filling the holy water stones with clean water before it had been hallowed every Sunday morning and locking the doors every night. In the pillar on the south side of the lantern was a stone containing twelve cresset lamps, which were lit every night to light the way for the monks coming to matins at midnight.

The North Transept had three altars in its east side, each with a window above, illustrating a scene from the life of the saint. The southernmost, dedicated to St Benedict, not only had a glorious window but also an elaborate screenwork around it with 'the order of St Bennett sett forth in these pictures in wainscott with a partition, the priors within and the monks without'. The 149 pictures of saints, each identified, must have formed a well-illustrated history of the Order of monks whose Convent this was. The northern light in the North Transept transmitted the four Doctors of the church, St Cuthbert, the Virgin Mary and, beneath her feet, a picture of Prior Castell holding up his hands to her, to those serving and worshipping at the altars, reminding them incidentally to pray for the soul of the Prior who had renovated the north window.

The South Transept was the richer of the two in appearance. Its southern window, called the 'Te Deum' window, was glazed 'accordinge as every verse of Te Deum is song or saide, so it is pictured in the wyndowe verie fynly and curioyslie wrowghte in fyne colored glass with all the nyne order of Angells . . . with the pictur of christ as he was upon the cross crucified, and the blessed Virgin Marie with crist in her armes as he was borne'. Below the window stood the clock built by Prior Castell.

Of the three altars in the east aisle of the transept the central, that dedicated to Our Lady of Bolton, was perhaps the most interesting. Erected at the expense of the Neville family, the altar supported a picture which, when closed, showed the Virgin Mary surrounded by a border of green paint decorated with flowers in gold. When opened it revealed the image of Christ 'most marveylouse fynlie gilted' holding up his hands, which had between them a large gold crucifix. This was taken forth every Good Friday 'and every man did crepe unto it that was in the church on that Daye'. On every principal day the image was opened 'that every man might se pictured within her, the father, the sonne, and the holy ghost, most curiouslye and fynlye gilted'.

The east end of the nave was closed by a high stone screen pierced by two doors on either side of the Jesus altar which was placed centrally against the west face. A triptych which portrayed the Passion in colours 'all like burninge gold' was opened only during mass. A wooden screen, painted red, enclosed the altar on its three open sides. It had four cupboards for vestments and altar furniture on the south side and a door in the centre of the west side topped by iron spikes to prevent people climbing in. The screen behind the altar had three friezes running the width of the nave. The lowest told the story of the Passion; above were the Apostles, and at the top a border painted with brilliant colours and finely gilted flowers and branches. Standing on top of this 'most goodly and famous Roode that was yn this land' was a series of statues. On the east face of the rood was a loft containing a clock and under the loft was a bench where men sat to rest and hear divine service.

Every Friday after evensong the choristers came into the nave and entered a loft between the two easternmost pillars on the north side. Accompanied by an organ there they sang an anthem. All the while the Galilee bells would toll.

The north aisle of the nave had a wooden trellice topped with iron spikes, reaching to the vault at the east end. A door of two leaves led into the North Transept, but that was only opened on holy days. The aisle was lit by three windows. There were but two altars in this aisle. The Chapel of Our Lady of Pity was between the pair of pillars immediately west of the door, and enclosed by a fine wooden screen. North of the entry into the Gaililee was St Saviour's altar, built into the wall. Stairs in the wall led up to the belfry in the Galilee steeple, in which hung four bells rung at Principal Feasts and when the Bishop came to Durham. On Sunday the great bell was tolled for three quarters of an hour after noon and rung for the last fifteen minutes before one o'clock, at which hour a sermon was preached in the Galilee until three.

The south aisle was lit by six windows. The roof of the easternmost bay was a wooden ceiling painted blue and spangled with stars. A holy water stone set between the two easternmost pillars and protected by a wall from the nave was covered by a wooden canopy painted blue in the midst of which was 'a great Starre of great Compasse like unto the sonne veri artificially & most Curiouslie gilt and ennamyled veri goodly to all the beholdres therof, so that there coulde no duste nor fylthe faule into the holy water stone yt was so close above head & so close within the church doure'. The holy water stone by the north door was also protected by a blue wooden canopy, less elaborately decorated.

The two bays immediately west of this elaborate canopy were occupied by the Neville Chantry. Bishop Robert Neville, John and Ralph, Lords Neville were all buried there. The Prior's pew facing into the nave was above Ralph's tomb.

At the west end of the aisle, opposite the altar of Our Lady of Pity, was the altar of the Bound Rood. Set in the south wall and opposite the altar of St Saviour was The Grate, a room where people claiming Sanctuary were housed and fed for thirty-seven days. Those claiming sanctuary had generally committed a 'grete crime' such as murder, horse or cattle stealing, escaping from prison or, on occasion, burglary. They came to Durham to claim immunity from secular law for thirty-seven days. If, within that period, they were unable to obtain a pardon, they were taken out of the Diocese, generally to a port where they could go overseas. The first records of Sanctuary granted by St Cuthbert's community were in the late ninth century, when they were still at Chester-le-Street. Once the new church had been built in Durham in the 11th-12th centuries, the sanctuary ring was fixed to the north door so that those claiming sanctuary could reach safety before entering the church. It is likely, however, that there was a sanctuary 'zone' around the Priory, which was defined by the series of crosses placed on all the main roads leading into Durham: Charley's Cross, Neville's Cross, etc.

Above the original west door of the nave was a large window containing the Tree of Jesse, which was inserted into the Norman west front in the time of Prior Fossour (1341-74). Later, Bishop Langley transplanted some of the Norman intersecting blank arcades to fill the doorway. The Galilee, west of the doorway, had four altars. The principal one, to the Virgin Mary, was lavish, being finely adorned with wooden panelling all round and above 'furnished with most heavenly pictures so lyvely in cullers and gilting'.

On the north side was an altar, probably dedicated to the Holy Cross, which had a magnificent painting on the wall behind it, which still partly survives. South of the central altar was the Venerable Bede's altar and shrine. The monument was of blue marble standing three feet high, supported on five pillars. Above it was a gold and silver shrine containing Bede's bones (removed from St Cuthbert's coffin and placed in the shrine by Bishop Pudsey). The saint's remains were probably translated to the Galilee in 1370 at the expense of Richard of Barnard Castle.

The west wall of the Galilee had a central window below which was an iron pulpit, from which a sermon was preached every Sunday and holy day at 1pm. In the southwest corner was the font for baptising infants. There were five windows in the west wall the glass of four of which was 'richly wrought with pictures and imagery of Saints'.

Outside the church, but remaining within the Convent, the cloister walks were enclosed in glass, painted to tell the whole story of St Cuthbert from birth to death, together with the miracles.

The cloister garth held two great structures. The laver where the monks washed their hands before eating stood against the south side of the garth near the refectory door. It was made of marble quarried from Egglestone in Teesdale and had eight sides, each having three bronze spouts leading water from the central reservoir to the outer face, where there was a trough to catch it. There was an outer stone wall which had seven windows; the eighth side was a door leading to the south cloister walk. The whole structure was topped by a dovecote with a leaden roof. When the monks had washed their hands and faces they dried them on towels 'kept alwaies . . . swete' in cupboards on either side of the refectory door.

The other structure in the cloister garth was a monument to St Cuthbert, which marked where his coffin had rested before the translation of his remains to the new shrine in 1104. Its base was a tomb (standing before the entry leading to the cemetery but within the area formerly occupied by the earlier church) which was three feet high, surmounted by a statue of the saint. To protect the statue from the weather there was a leaden roof supported by timber uprights, which were positioned so closely together that the curious 'man coulde not have gotten in his hand betwixt one stanchell & another'.

Without the life of St Cuthbert in the early years of Christianity in this country, the whole history of County Durham would have been different, for it would never have attained its status of a kingdom within a kingdom without the generous land grants made to St Cuthbert and his servants. Indeed, since his Convent occupies the best-defended area of the peninsula, which might otherwise have been occupied by a town, he effectively determined the form of Durham City. The Convent was centred on St Cuthbert's shrine. Pilgrims, including kings and queens, came from far afield to pay homage (there was a small locked box with two slits in it for the reception of coins). Canute came, as Robert Hegge tells us in his inimitable way, 'in an excess of devotion' from Garmondsway 'five miles barefoote to *St Cuthbert's* Tombe, and as if he meant to make satisfaction for the wrong his Ancestors had done to that Saint, he gave him soe many Townes as would breath a fatt monk to repeat them . . .'.

The shrine to which the Saint was removed in 1104 was probably a fairly simple one, but as time went on the fittings became increasingly elaborate, particularly in the fourteenth century, when John, Lord Neville, paid £200 for a new gilded marble stone on which to place three nesting coffins in their shrine as well as the magnificent reredos to the high altar. There was an altar at the west end of the shrine where mass was said on St Cuthbert's day in Lent. At this feast and on certain other days the cover of the shrine was raised so that people could see inside. The cover, painted red within, had an iron rod fixed in the marble beneath and driven through each corner to guide it when lifted by means of a silken cord and pulley. The shrine that was visible to pilgrims as they knelt in the four niches in the marble support had some magnificent paintings on it. The top was covered with 'carved worke cutt owte with Dragons and other beasts moste artificially wroughte . . .'.

It seems that St Cuthbert was not alone in his coffin for, even in 1104, when the coffin was opened before the translation, were found 'the Booke of the Evangelists which had fallen into the Sea, a little Silver Altar, a Goblet of pure Gold, with an Onix stone, and an Ivory Combe in the 2nd (coffin)'. In the third and innermost coffin were found 'the Body of their Saint (which the Grave in soe many yeares had not digested) lying upon his right side to give room

41

for the rest of the Reliques'. These included the Venerable Bede, the head of St Oswald and part of the bones of Aidan, Eadfrid and Ethelwold, all Bishops of Lindisfarne. Now, there was not one, but several inspections of the contents of the coffin immediately before the translation in 1104. The first was carried out by Prior Turgot and nine chosen monks.

They found the saint incorrupt together with the large number of relics which have already been described. They took St Cuthbert out and put the relics to one side before returning him to the coffin. When they reported this happy state of affairs to Bishop Ralph, he refused to believe them. On the next night, the monks repeated the removal of the saint's remains from the coffin and then wrapped his body in additional vestments before returning it once again to the coffin with only the head of St Oswald from among all the other relics. The Translation was quite clearly an important event, for large numbers of visitors were in Durham to witness it. The Durham monks were then told by a visiting abbot that they should have told others what they were doing and should have had other witnesses than themselves, else they could be accused of falsifying the evidence for the incorruption of St Cuthbert. The monks, much perturbed by this, arranged for yet another disturbance of the remains. At this exhumation were present the Abbot of St Albans, the Abbot of St Mary, York, and Hugh, Abbot of St German. In addition, Alexander, brother of the King of Scotland was present as well as William, the Bishop's clerk who later became Archbishop of Canterbury. Only the Abbot of Seez was allowed to touch the remains once they had been exposed. Once he had declared that the body was indeed incorrupt, the translation was allowed to proceed.

Many of the relics had been collected by a monk called Elfred, a member of the secular community in the early eleventh century. He had, as often as not, obtained them by stealth. The most blatant example was his removal of the remains of the Venerable Bede in their entirety from Jarrow under cover of darkness. They had been displayed in the church at Jarrow every year on the anniversary of Bede's death.

Many people gave relics to the shrine. In 1383 a huge list of the relics was compiled. It included the proven remains, of a number of griffin's eggs, the head of St Aidan ornamented with copper gilt and precious stones and such a quantity of assorted relics as makes Hegge's description of this same list seem modest by comparison:

'. . . I find a Catalogue of the *Reliques* of this Abby, which were soe many, that it seem'd a Charnell house of Saints Bones; for from hence at the Resurrection *St Stephen* will fetch his Tooth, *Zachary* a Leg; *Simon* an Arme; *St Christopher* an Elbow, *St Lawrence* a Finger, *St Ambrose* some of his Haire, *St Ebbe* her Foote, with many more; besides an whole Wardrop of Saint's Apparell, both of Coats and Hoods, and Stockens of the Apostles, with diverse fractions of the Crosse and the sacred Sepulchre' not to mention the tooth of St Gengulphus, said to be good for the falling sickness, and kept in a small ivory pyx with three feet.

The dissolution of the monastery saw the dismantling of the shrine in November 1541. The marble was removed in that month and St Cuthbert's remains were moved to the vestry. On New Year's Day 1542 George Skeles was paid 15d for 2½ days' work for making the grave of St Cuthbert. It was not until 17 May 1827 that St Cuthbert was again disturbed. This scientific exhumation, under the direction of Rev James Raine, established that the 1542 grave was covered with a large slab sealed by eighteen inches of earth and a marble slab presently visible in the floor. Three nesting coffins were found, the innermost being the original coffin marvellously carved. Inside it were the bones of St Cuthbert dressed in vestments and wrapped in fine linen. At least five silk garments were identified, of which one was probably put on the saint during his temporary removal from the shrine, when the Chapel of the Nine Altars was built in the thirteenth century, two were put on in the 1104 translation while the remaining two, a stole and maniple, were the gift of King Athelstan (924-940). Additionally, an Ivory Comb, Silver Altar and purse were found in the coffin. On the saint's breast was a gold pendant cross inset with garnets and hung about the neck with a silken cord. All of these, together with the coffin with its vibrant carvings can still be seen in the Cathedral Treasury.

At the exhumation in 1827, Raine concluded that the community had deliberately falsified the evidence for the incorruption from as early as 698. However, a subsequent exhumation allowed a more detailed and leisurely examination of the remains. It was concluded that St Cuthbert's body had indeed been incorrupt since portions of skin, ligaments and other parts of the body were still intact. It seems that St Cuthbert was first interred in such a dry part of the ground that his body was dessicated.

Presumably the incorrupt remains of a saint were worth more to the Convent in terms of income from pilgrims, than those that were only bones. Indeed, St Cuthbert's shrine was an extremely wealthy one, even when the huge land grants made to his community are ignored. Pilgrims provided a steady income for many years, but this started to diminish in the 15th century and appears to have ceased altogether by the 16th. The bones of an eminent saint could, nevertheless, be of considerable profit to the Convent, especially when they belonged to the Venerable Bede. On the exhumation of his remains in 1830, it was found that very few bones remained. The majority were to be found in a multitude of churches both in England and in Europe, and had presumably changed hands to the profit of Durham Priory.

The Reformation saw the present Dean and Chapter arise from the scarcely-cold ashes of the dissolved monastery, an organisational change accompanied by the removal of altars and shrines but little else besides. The compiler of *The Rites of Durham*, composing that indispensable description of the monastic Convent, must still have had acts of the Calvinist Deans Horne and Whittingham (the latter not only married to Calvin's sister but also a co-translator of the Geneva Bible) burned on his memory, if the intermperate language that he uses to describe their activities is any guide. They are charged with destroying the shrine and statue of St Cuthbert that stood in the cloister garth and with smashing painted glass and other images. Both seem to have had an aversion to images; Whittingham, in particular, seems to have been 'religiously loath . . . that any monument of St Cuthbert, or of any man (who formerly had beene famous in this church and great benefactors thereunto, as the priors and his predecessors were) should be left whole and undefaced . . .'. More particularly Whittingham and his wife took the holy water stones — presumably lying unused in or about the church — for use in steeping salt fish and beef 'havinge a conveiance in the bottomes of them for letting furth the water, as thei had when they weare in the church. And the greater holie water stone is removed into the lower end of the Deanes Buttire where the water Counditt is sett, & next unto the wyne seller, wher in now their wash and make cleane ther potts and cuppes before they serve theme at the table'.

There seems to have been relatively little additional damage to the Cathedral until 1650 (the demolition of the Sacrist's Exchequer in 1637 excepted) when the church was used as a prison for some 3,000 of the 5,000 Scottish prisoners of war taken at the battle of Dunbar. They had been marched from the battlefield to Durham and arrived in poor condition. They were not supplied with coal or wood for fires and generally suffered from the maladministration of 'one Brewen, appointed to looke to the Scotts . . . a man of badd conscience and a cruell fellowe to the poore prisoners . . . most of them perished and dyed ther in a very short space, and were thrown into holes by great numbers together, in a most lamentable manner'. To keep themselves warm the prisoners burned all the available wood they could find, thereby destroying most, if not all, of the medieval woodwork in the church. They are also said to have almost destroyed the Neville monuments in the Neville chantry chapel. Seven years later, the lead-covered wooden spires on the western towers were taken down.

Between them, John Cosin (Bishop 1660-73) and John Sudbury (Dean 1661-84) set about making good the damage of the preceding century. Dean Sudbury at his own considerable expense rebuilt the refectory as a library which is still there today and repaired the Deanery. John Cosin, among a number of other works in the county, erected the existing stalls in the choir and had the font cover made anew. This work was probably done by James Clement, who died in 1690 and was buried in St Oswald's Church. Among these works must be included the small organ bought and installed by Cosin in 1661 and another paid for by Dean Barwick and working by St Stephen's Day 1662. There had been silence for twenty-one years, as the Scots had destroyed the earlier organ cases in 1650.

The main organ built for Cosin and Barwick only survived until 1683, when an agreement was reached between the Dean and Chapter and Bernard (Father) Smith to build a new one costing £700. This was completed by 1687 and, despite alterations, was still in its place over the choir screen door in 1846, when it was moved to the north side of the choir as the screen was taken down. The reason behind this alteration was that 'the organ screen, however much admired as a work of art, was universally condemned, its debased style of architecture being inappropriate to a Norman edifice'. Similar arguments applied to the choir screen as a whole which was 'of dark oak, divided into compartments by pilasters of Italian character, assuming the form of caryatides, and adorned with a profusion of carving representing fruit and flowers, in bold relief, displaying considerable skill in the execution and possessing much richness of effect.'. The organ survived until 1873, when it was deemed beyond further repair and was replaced by a new one built by Willis of London. Part of the Smith organ case survives in the church, and is thought to have part of Cosin's choir screen still attached.

Extensive and largely destructive, if not architecturally misleading, renovation and rebuilding occurred in the late 18th and 19th centuries. The Chapter House was the principal loss, being a completely Norman structure, the eastern portion of which was demolished in 1796. The following year proposals to replace the Galilee with a sweeping carriage way to the Norman west entrance were fortunately confounded, though not before the lead was off the roof. Right at the end of the 19th century the Chapter House was rebuilt on the lines of its Norman forbear, fortunately not before the opportunity had been taken to excavate the ground, thereby showing that the Norman apsed building had had a square-ended predecessor in the 1070s or 1080s.

In 1844 one of the few suriving relics of the medieval church, Prior Castell's clock (admittedly refurbished by Dean Hunt), was disembowelled and parts encased in the wall. It had earlier been connected to the chimes in the tower by John Bolton, the quarter hours being struck for the first time on Christmas Eve, 1808. However, it was rescued and rebuilt in 1938 and put back where it belongs, gracing the South Transept below the Te Deum window.

Since then there have been a number of repair campaigns, the most disastrous being that of Gilbert Scott, with the introduction of the present choir screen, if that is the appropriate description for the hoops that cross the west end of the choir. As time has passed, so those responsible for the maintenance of the Cathedral have taken a firm grasp of their responsibilities, so that today we may be sure the structure we have inherited will survive. One must, however, regret the unsympathetic way in which the Norman bolts holding the Sanctuary Knocker were sawn through when it was removed in 1980 for conservation. The Knocker and other treasures of the Cathedral are preserved and displayed in the Dormitory undercroft in the west claustral range.

ABOVE: Part of a page from an 11th century Antiphonal, probably written in north France and used in the Priory in the time of Bishop William of St Calais; the marks above the text indicate pitch for singing. LEFT: A page from an 8th century Northumbrian Gospel containing Jesus' Genealogy (Luke: 3) with musical notation above the words. (DC A.II.17) RIGHT: The Sanctuary Knocker on the north door of the nave (the original is now on display in the Treasury in the dormitory undercroft). (DC)

ABOVE and OPPOSITE: Wall paintings in the north aisle of the Galilee.
(DC) LEFT: One of the ends of St Cuthbert's coffin decorated with an
incised drawing of the Virgin and Child. RIGHT: Pectoral cross found
with St Cuthbert when his coffin was opened in 1827. (Both DC)

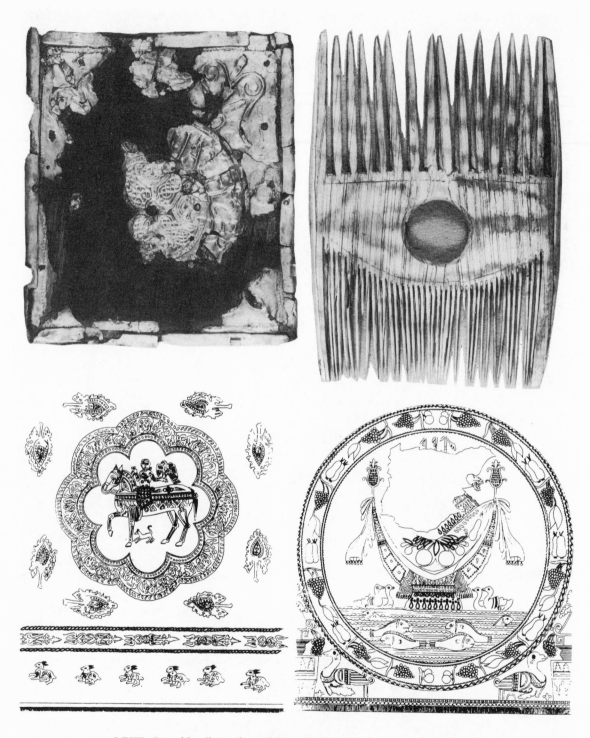

LEFT: Portable silver alter (DC) and RIGHT: ivory comb, from the saint's coffin. (DC) BELOW: Patterns from the richly embroidered silk coverings added to St Cuthbert's wrappings during the 1104 Translation.

LEFT: 10th century maniple made for Bishop Frithstan on the order of
Aelfled, queen of Edward the Elder and placed in St Cuthbert's coffin at
a subsequent date. (DC) RIGHT: Prior Castell's clock in the South
Transept in 1929. (DUAD)

49

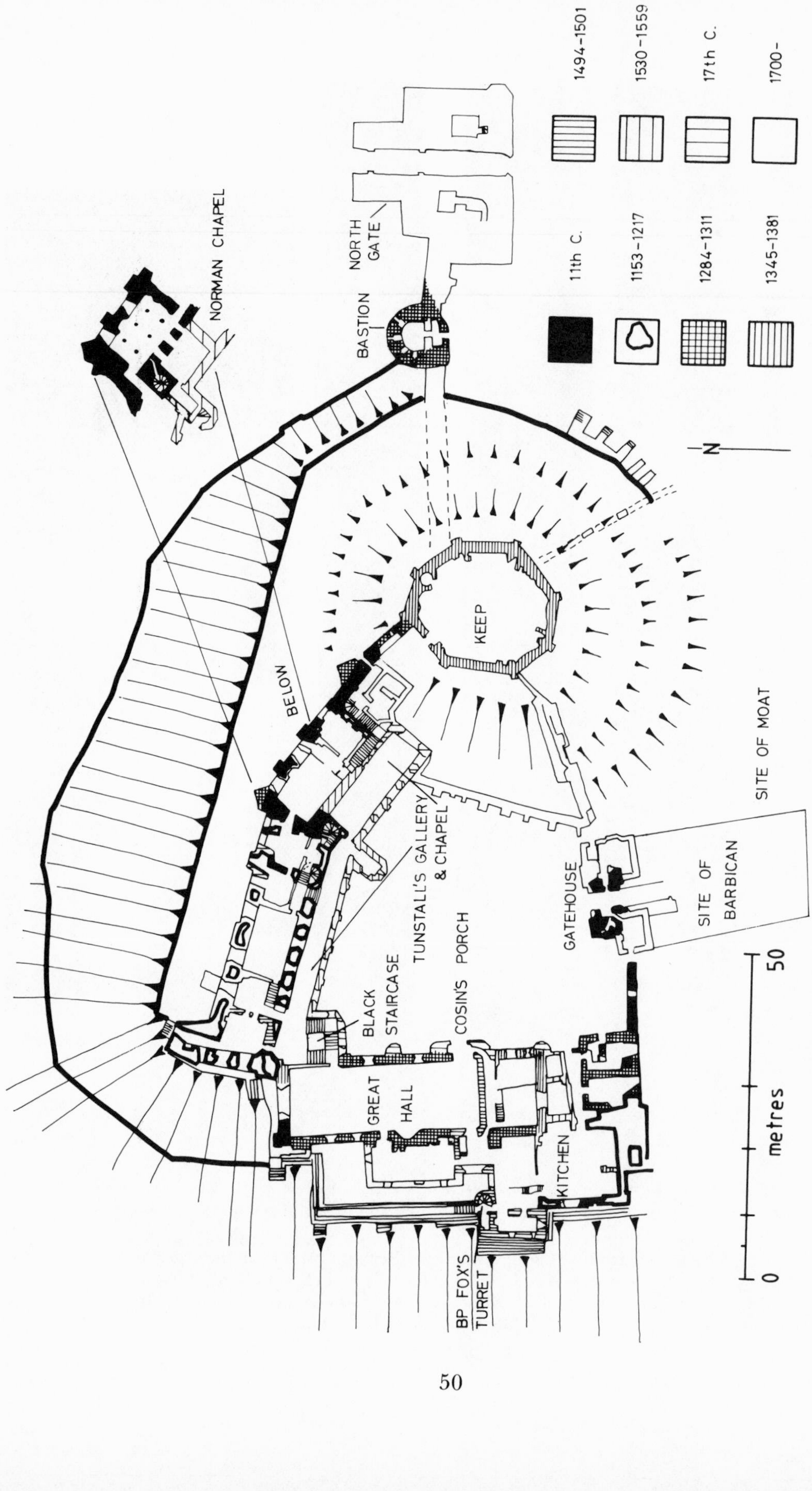

Plan of the Castle's Inner Bailey.

Legend:

11th C.	1494–1501
1153–1217	1530–1559
1284–1311	17th C.
1345–1381	1700–

NORMAN CHAPEL

BASTION

NORTH GATE

KEEP

BELOW

TUNSTALL'S GALLERY & CHAPEL

COSIN'S PORCH

BLACK STAIRCASE

GREAT HALL

KITCHEN

BP FOX'S TURRET

GATEHOUSE

SITE OF BARBICAN

SITE OF MOAT

N

metres

0   50

The Bishop's Castle

Durham Castle in 995 was no more than an earthen rampart topped by a timber palisade. It may simply have been on the northern limits of the peninsular plateau, or — more likely in view of the unsuccessful Scottish siege of 1040 — it circumscribed the whole of the plateau, thereby protecting not just St Cuthbert's church and community, but also the town. The heads of the slain Scots were displayed on poles in the Market Place in the area of the present Palace Green.

Robert Cumin came to Durham in January 1069 as the Earl of Northumberland, appointed by William and accompanied by seven hundred soldiers, to help enforce his acceptance by the Northumbrians. He ignored a warning that they were plotting against his life and settled in the town. Early next morning (31 January) the mob broke the gates and murdered the soldiers. Those who escaped made for the Bishop's house, where Cumin was staying. The mob set fire to the house and slew all except one. While the building was burning, sparks rose into the air and threatened the western tower of the church. The people went on their knees and 'besought St Cuthbert to preserve his church from burning; and immediately a wind arose from the east which drove the flames backwards from the church and entirely freed it from danger. The house, however, which had caught fire continued to blaze; and of those persons who were in it some were burnt and some were slaughtered as they crossed its doors. Thus' says Symeon, 'the earl was put to death, along with all of his followers, save one who escaped wounded'.

The King's response was swift and savage, for he devastated the land between York and Durham in 1070. Symeon, probably overstating the case somewhat, says that 'between York and Durham he did not leave a house standing, reducing the whole district by fire and sword, to a horrible desert smoking with blood and in ashes'. Two years later the King ordered the construction of a castle at Durham, on his return from wars in Scotland. From then to 1096 an annual payment from the revenues of Waltham Abbey was made towards the cost of this work. The Castle was defensible by 1075; Archbishop Lanfranc ordered Bishop Walcher to furnish it with men, arms and provisions in preparation for a Danish attack.

Today little survives of the earliest work, and most of that under the motte or later Norman work. Perhaps the most enchanting piece of Norman architecture on the peninsula is in the chapel. Small, and with a flagged floor, the piers supporting the low vaulted roof have capitals from which bound some wonderful beasts in a hunting scene, as well as faces and leaves. This formed part of a larger building, some of which may now be partly buried under the spread earthen mound on which Hatfield's keep was built. The basement of the Great Hall on the west side of the inner enclosure is also witness to the extent of the first Castle, with small windows belonging to that period. A flagged floor and a wall, perhaps part of the first Castle, were found below the floor in 1932.

Bishop Flambard (1099-1128) is said to have built a 'strong and loftier wall' around the City. This might either mean that he replaced a wall erected by his immediate predecessors, or that he replaced the original defences that had merely been tinkered with, while building the Castle's inner defences. Whichever is true, he certainly concentrated his works on the outer defences, building a new additional wall from the keep to the east end of the church. The dwellings of the townspeople had been cleared away, in order, says the Chronicler 'that the church should neither be endangered by fire nor polluted by filth'. This was fair comment, since the town had been set afire at some point between 1096 and 1099.

The Castle, even in Flambard's time, was a multiple-enclosured defensive system. It had a keep on a mound as the eccentric citadel of the triangular inner bailey, which was itself defended by a moat and barbicaned gate. The walled enclosure between the Convent and Castle that once held the town communicated with the outer enclosure by two gates (Owengate and Lyegate — *Le Lycheyate* in 1340). Indeed it now held all the principal administrative buildings for the Bishopric as well as the mint. The Convent itself was a further walled enclosure in two parts: the conventual buildings turned in on themselves, and their store buildings ranged round what is now The College, and communicating with the outer enclosure through Abbey Gate. The whole was defended on the south and east by an outer walled enclosure, now the North and South Baileys. Regrettably little of the walls survives. The only gate still standing is the Abbey Gate, leading from the South Bailey into the conventual 'outer bailey', filled with store buildings of one sort or another around an open space.

The central triangular enclosure of the Castle held the keep on its high earthen mound in one corner. From Prior Laurence's mid-twelfth century description, it was a timber structure with an octagonal stone skin, connected to the walls of both the inner and outer enclosures. Indeed, one of the eight faces of the keep actually formed part of the northern wall of the inner enclosure. This was lower than the keep, and
'contains beautiful structures.
It displays two great adjoining palaces with porticoes, in which art itself sufficiently attests the artificers.
Here also the Chaple is conspicuous, supported on six columns, not too spacious, but sufficiently handsome.
Here chambers are joined to chambers and buildings to buildings, and to each is assigned its own function.
Here garments, there vessels shine; here arms gleam; here money lies hid; here is flesh; there is bread.
Here grain, there wine lies; here beer made of oats; here also the clean flour has its proper place.
And although on this side houses are thus joined to houses, and buildings to buildings, yet on the other no part is vacant.
The middle of the castle is not occupied by buildings but that place exhibits a deep well of abundant water.'

While the outer wall ran round the top of the cliffs, it was pierced by several posterns or sallyports: Kingsgate by St Mary-le-Bow church, Baileygate at the southern limit of the South Bailey and Windy Gap, the two former leading to fords across the river while the last, together with the Prior's postern, the 'Dark Entry', led to the Priory mill as well as to Framwellgate Bridge, which was built as part of the relocation of the town by Flambard. It provided convenient and defensible access, from the Great North Road on the west side of the river, to the newly built but undefended town below the Castle. The main gate in the outer defences was the North Gate. It is described by Laurence as having a tower over it, seemingly larger than other towers in the defensive enciente; there was also a wall on either side, leading to the keep to the west and the river on the east. There was an open space on the north side of the gate with a slope to the river 'steep and rough and high; it is also uneven; neither is it well adapted for horses'. The Castle side of this open space was, of course, defended by the Castle itself.

In the early years of the episcopate of Hugh of le Puiset, a fire raged in the town so fiercely that it consumed many of the houses, and destroyed the internal buildings of the Castle itself. They were rebuilt by the Bishop, together with sections of the outer wall. The core of the north range is identifiable as his work, as also a part of what is now the kitchen at the south end of the range. Le Puiset's buildings were generally attractive, though perhaps one of the most elegant must be the long bridge of 14 arches (according to Leland) rising from the borough of Elvet to join Fleshergate and Saddler Street on the peninsula.

The west range of the Castle, then as now the Great Hall, was built by Bishop Bek (1284-1311) and rebuilt and enlarged by Bishop Hatfield (1345-81), whose contract with John Alverton, made in 1351, survives. Alverton, a carpenter, was to rebuild the hall and to re-use timbers from the old hall, discounting that to the final agreed cost of £45. The hall that was being replaced was scarcely small, for on the day that Bishop Bury was enthroned in 1333, he entertained the King and Queen of England, the Dowager Queen of England, the King of Scotland, two archbishops, five bishops, seven earls and their ladies, all the nobility from north of the Trent and 'a vast concourse of knights, esquires, and other people of distinction, among whom were many abbots, priors and other religious'.

Hatfield's enormous hall was later considerably altered by Bishop Fox (1494-1501) who curtailed the lower, southern end, and converted that to kitchens, buttery and pantries. His hatches and wooden partitions still survive with later additions, as well as the huge fireplaces in the kitchen. The present portico to the Great Hall, with four buttresses on the south side, was added by Bishop Cosin.

The keep was rebuilt by Bishop Hatfield, perhaps using the earlier foundations, on its octagonal plan with five stairs in the angles. He also re-edified parts of the north range, in particular the north wall. Even in Bishop Tunstall's time (1530-1559) the north and west ranges were separate buildings. He increased the width of the north range by a half when he added a series of apartments with a gallery over, and a chapel at the first floor on the east end. His new entry to the range obscured Bishop Puiset's masterpiece, the grand doorway into his hall. Tunstall's chapel was enlarged by Bishop Cosin who, in the 1660s, saw the convenience of connecting the two ranges by an enclosed stair, now known as the Black Stair, in the angle between them.

The Scots army under Robert de Brus came south of the Anglo-Scottish border in August 1312 and, after causing much devastation in Northumberland and Cumberland, crossed the Tyne and attacked Durham, seizing everything possible and then firing the town. In the following year, Bishop Kellawe ordered an Inquisition into the value of properties to be removed near the Northgate, preparatory to the reconstruction of the North Gate barbican.

Those who survived the murderous attack petitioned the King in 1315 for permission to erect a town wall. A tower was built at the west end of Elvet Bridge, another across Claypath immediately north of St Nicholas church and, on the river bank west of St Nicholas, a further one. Walls connected the Castle's North Gate to Elvet Bridge and thence along the top of the slope, turning at right angles to join Claypath Gate, crossing the ridge, and reaching the river near Walkergate. The wall then ran along the river's edge. The stone wall, presently visible at the bottom of the riverside walls in Fowler's Yard, almost certainly forms part of the City wall. The final encirclement of the City was the tower with drawbridge and small barbican, standing on the east end of Franwellgate Bridge. A further wall connected this tower to the Castle defences and may be coeval with the bridge and its tower.

The short length of City wall revealed during the excavations of Fowler's Yard was about five or six feet thick and stood nearly twenty feet high. It had been patched and repaired from time to time and showed a walkway near the top, on which a later wall had been built, to be finally covered with soil and rubbish accumulating from inside the town during the seventeenth and eighteenth centuries. The need for constant repairs is shown in the grants of tolls specifically for walls and paving. There were three such grants in less than a century after the walls had been built, the earliest in 1337 and the two others in 1379 and 1407.

After the King had complained about the state of the defences in 1322-3, the North Gate was strengthened by the addition of a round bastion on the outer face of the wall leading up to the Castle. At this point, bastion and walls will have stood some sixty feet above the then ground level. Presumably the North Gate stood to that height as well, thus forming a formidable defence at the entrance to the Castle. However, by the mid-fourteenth century, its defensive value was somewhat reduced since individuals were able to lease and seemingly build on land immediately adjacent to the walls both inside and outside the Castle. There is a suggestion, too, that the land in the North Bailey had not been fully colonised by buildings until the mid-fourteenth century, for in 1340 John de Ferow was able to lease a row of newly built houses extending from the gate called *Le Licheyate* (Lyegate) as far as the manse of the Archdeacons of Durham. These buildings are described as being beside the stone wall (presumably Flambard's wall from the keep to the east end of the church). Since this property is described as in the Bailey rather than on Palace Green, it seems probable that the houses lay on the east side of the wall, (and the west side of the road now called North Bailey).

Bishop Langley completely rebuilt the North Gate in the few years before 1421. He probably rebuilt within the limits of the earlier gate but made it more defensible, with an outer gate with portcullis facing the town and, at the south end of the barbican, a double gate with a tower over. Internally there were all the normal features suitable for discomfitting attackers. The old gaol buildings on Palace Green were swept away in the time of Bishop Neville, not many years after the erection of the North Gate, and the gate in its turn served as the prison until 1820.

It seems strange that, Langley having rebuilt the North Gate on a magnificent scale in the second decade of the 15th century, Robert Rhodes was able to lease a property in the South Bailey in 1449, which allowed him powers to open or close the Water Gate at will. This gate survived until about 1780, when it was taken down and rebuilt to accommodate a wider roadway, by Rev Henry Egerton, who enjoyed the same property and privilege as Robert Rhodes. This gate gave access to a ferry in the 13th or 14th centuries, replaced by a stake and plank footbridge in 1574, whose successor of 1778 stands a little downstream today.

The decay of the walls and towers of the Castle and City was a long process. By the last decade of the 16th century both Owengate and Lyegate had gone. Robert Hegge in 1626 refers to 'the ruine of her Walls'. During the next century much of the outer Castle wall, with its buttresses and interval towers and the postern at Kingsgate had gone, or been subsumed within other buildings. At No 2 North Bailey the occupants had dumped their rubbish over the wall in the earlier 17th century but, in the early years of the 18th, it was completely removed to make way for a new building, which completely ignored its line. The rear of No 4 North Bailey is built on the remains of an interval tower. Walkergate seems to have been removed in the course of the 17th or 18th centuries, though vestiges survived until about 1940.

The three remaining gates were all victims of road improvements. Framwellgate Bridge Gate came down in 1760 'for the convenience of carriages'. Claypath Gate was demolished in 1791 'being adjudged a nuisance'. The North Gate might still be there today were it not made redundant as a gaol when the New Prison was built in Elvet, and demolished in 1820.

The 18th century also saw improvements to the Castle buildings, making them fit for bishops to occupy. This was in spite of the large scale work of Bishops Cosin and Crewe, who made good the ravages of the Mayor of London's occupation in the 1650s, when he bought the Castle during its sequestration by Parliament. The keep, however, had been adjudged ruinous by the 1630s, and nothing had been done about it. An empty shell, it stood four storeys high, with vaults still in place. The parapet was defended by an embattled breastwork, taken down in 1789 by order of Bishop Thurlow. So matters continued, until the Castle passed into the University's hands, when the only possible action was taken. 'The old keep, with its shattered and broken outline, shaggy with ivy, was perhaps a more picturesque object, but none can regret the purpose to which it is now applied [the University] or do otherwise than admire the skill [of Salvin] displayed in the re-edification of its massy walls' in 1840. In other words, the keep was rebuilt on the lines of its predecessor.

Eighty years later it was found that the Castle's original builders had built on sand, and that the whole edifice was in danger of cracking apart and descending either onto the town, or into the Wear. International help allowed the necessary work to proceed during the 1930s, when the massive structure was underpinned, using mining techniques, driving drifts in from the banks, and the walls held together with ties and concrete forced in under pressure.

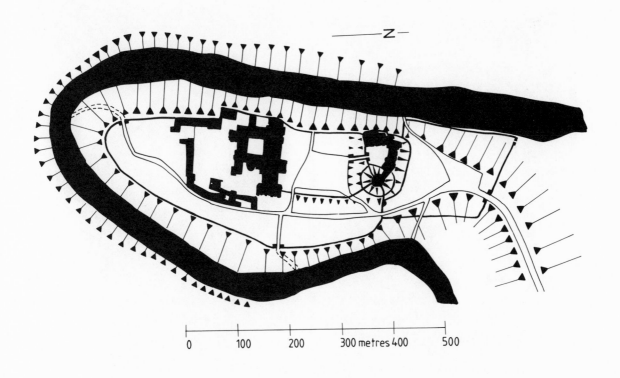

Plan of Durham's defence.

South west view of Durham Castle by Samuel and Nathaniel Buck in 1728. LEFT: Portrait of (later Prior) Laurence the monk . (DUL Cosin MS V.III.1,f22v) CENTRE: Norman capital found in the foundations of the Norman gallery, c1930. BELOW: Detail of capital in the Norman Chapel. (All DUAD)

ABOVE: West face of the Castle photographed from Framwellgate
Bridge in 1930. LEFT: South end (Bishop Fox's Gallery), and RIGHT:
north end, of the Great Hall. (DUAD)

OPPOSITE ABOVE LEFT: Norman drain discovered inside the castle; RIGHT: the Norman Gallery in 1928. CENTRE: 13th century semi-circular bastion under repair: note the reinforcing rods, 1932; BELOW: the bastion repaired, 1932. (All DUAD) LEFT: South face of the North Gate before its demolition in 1820, Joseph Bouet RIGHT: looking northwards through it. (DC Add MS 95) BELOW: Bishop Fox's Buttery, 1883.

South face of the North Gate, T. M. Richardson, 1881.

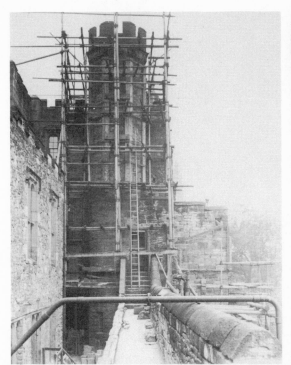

LEFT: Repair work in progress on Bishop Fox's turret, 1935. BELOW:
Roof of Cosin's Black Staircase. RIGHT: Window of the Black Staircase
before repair. (All DUAD)

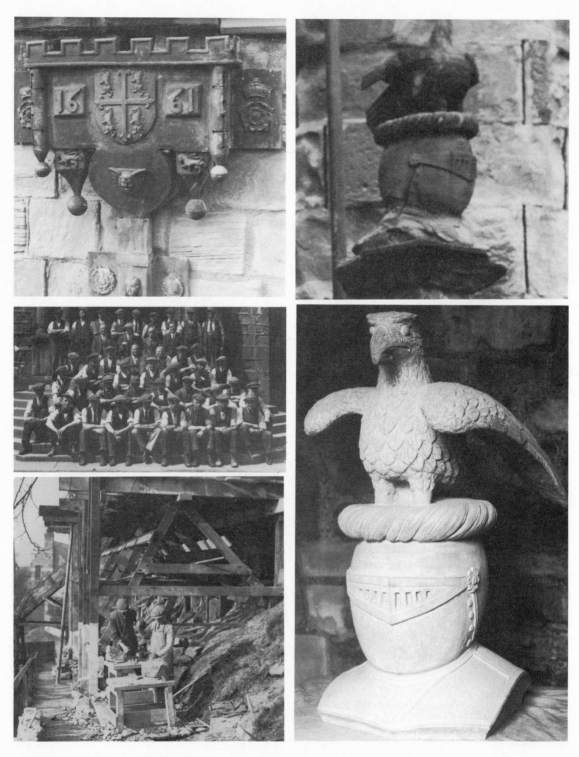

ABOVE LEFT: One of Bishop Cosin's rainwater hoppers; RIGHT: crest above Bishop Cosin's porch to the Great Hall before repair, and after. CENTRE: The men carrying out the repairs to the Castle, July 1931 and BELOW: masons at work (All DUAD).

ABOVE: Pressure grouting, 1929. BELOW: Drilling, 1929. (Both DUAD)

Repairing the wall between the Gatehouse and the Keep. (DUAD)

A City Chartered

There was a settlement at Elvet before the colonisation of the peninsular plateau in 995. The town of Durham with its market place was safely within the Castle walls until the time of Bishop Ralph Flambard (1099-1128). Even by the 1040s, it was a town, since it had a market place. At some point in Flambard's episcopate, the town in its entirety was moved down to the area around the present market place — not to Framwellgate.

Of the two reasons behind the 'new' site, the first was that the Bishop moved the town from one piece of his land to another, thereby keeping the revenues in his hands. After the 1083 division of St Cuthbert's lands between Bishop and Priory, the Priory had the lands off the peninsula (except Framwellgate) and the Bishop retained the peninsula (except the Convent area).

The second is the evidence provided by the excavation of Nos 61-3 Saddler Street. Here, there were three distinct periods of occupation, each having several phases within it. The first period, dated to the 10th-11th centuries, had one house on it replaced three times. The last replacement house was destroyed by fire. In the first phase a storm drain had carried water away from the site, but this soon became choked with scrap leather and domestic refuse, and was later covered by three successive middens of the same. It is likely that the houses were dwellings doubling as workshops, and were the source of all the material in the middens. At the end of this period the whole site was levelled with clay and sand, and three plots defined by post-and-rail fences, aligned at right angles to the present street line. The successors to these boundaries were still in place, vertically above the first fences, when the site was excavated in 1974. While structures are present in the three plots, they are not dwellings but sheds, a bread oven, middens and cess- and rubbish-pits. Indeed, one of the plots served as a vennel for a time in the second period (11th-12th centuries).

The second period on the site, with two or three separate phases on each plot, is dated to the 11th-12th centuries. The third period, which only occurs on one of the plots, is dated to the 12th-13th centuries. Throughout the three periods of occupation, leather was worked primarily for making and repairing shoes.

It is the change in the plots, seemingly in the late 11th or early 12th century that is important. Not only are three plots firmly defined simultaneously, but there is a change in their organisation, with dwellings placed at the front and ancillary buildings at the back. It suggests that a hand superior to that of the individual tenement-holder was at work, and one need look no further than Bishop Flambard's relocation of the town in the early 12th century. If this is so, then the Period 1 structures should perhaps be seen as representative of houses and workshops peripheral to the town, within the Castle, which straggled alongside the access routes to the prime area. The Period 2 (11th-12th century) structures belong to the relocated, newly-built town. One can imagine the Bishop's officers and representatives of the townspeople haggling over where the individual plots were to go; what the dimensions were to be and who was to have which plot. The overall layout of the new town will have been determined by the topography of the site.

There were two existing routes, one possibly more important than the other. The less important ran down the ridge, of which the peninsula was the termination. The more important was that running up from the western river crossing, presumably a ford in the late 11th century, but bridged by the Bishop as part of his town relocation. The route up from the bridge (Framwellgate Bridge) can hardly have been altered, for to have made it more direct would have resulted in such a steep gradient, that only goats could have used it. To have softened the gradient would have made the route over-long, perhaps reaching the top of the ridge somewhere north of St Nicholas church. Elvet at this date had access to Durham directly by a ford under the Kingsgate postern and, more convenient though less direct, round the southern end of the peninsula and across Framwellgate Bridge. No doubt, once the town had moved, there was a new ford further upstream to connect the two.

The Market Place was on the only piece of flat land in the town, with the houses on its east and west sides perched on the brink of a precipice above the river. St Nicholas Church, perhaps built when the town was moved, marked the northern limit of both market and town, while the Castle wall, marking the foot of the cliff, also formed the back of the house plots on the south side of the Market Place, as well as those on the south side of Silver Street.

Bishop Hugh of Le Puiset granted a charter to the City in 1180, allowing it markets, fairs and various freedoms. The grant of markets was clearly retrospective for there had been markets in Durham from at least 1040 and probably before. This charter was probably no more than the recognition of the existence of the City as an entity separate from the Castle. Nevertheless, he and his successors controlled the City through their own officers — bailiffs, stewards and clerks of the markets — until the seventeenth century. The Tollbooth, placed in the market place, was the focus of all this jurisdiction. In 1617 it was replaced by a market cross moved from Maids Arbour, a flat piece of ground at the east end of Gilesgate between the Sunderland and Sherburn Roads. Bishop Tunstall had built the Tollbooth on the west side of the market place by then . The erection of this cross is recorded in the Order Book of the Corporation of Durham in 1617. 'To the honor of Almightie God the ornament of the Cittie of Duresme and commoditie of the people frequentinge the market of Duresme, the market Crosse now there extant was framed with Twelve stone pillers and covered with lead at the sole charges and expenses of Thomas Emmerson of the blackFryers in London Esquier in the yere of our Lord one thousand six hundrethe and seaventene And in the fiftenthe yeare of the ragne of our soverayne Lord James by grace of God of England France and Ireland Kinge, defender of the faithe . . .'. The ancient cross was removed in 1780 and its materials used to erect a Piazza of nine arches used as the corn market.

Gilesgate had become a borough by the late twelfth century. In 1112 Bishop Flambard established a church and hospital dedicated to St Giles at the top of the long, rising ridge leading north-east from Durham. This he endowed with the vill of Caldecotes, believed to have been in the immediate vicinity, and a mill on the Milneburn, which formed the boundary between Framwellgate and the Old Borough (or Crossgate) on the west side of the Wear. The hospital attracted a small settlement within a short time.

St Giles suffered in the armed dispute between the usurper Bishop William Cumin and William of St Barbe, Bishop of Durham proper, which lasted for three years. In 1143 the Bishop and his supporters, led by Robert Conyers, advanced on Durham from their stronghold at Bishopton, attacked the Castle without success, and withdrew to St Giles. The chronicler described how Cumin 'then ordered the soldiers whom he had about him to sally out and attack the Bishop's men, who betook themselves to St Giles Church, at some distance from the walls, and stayed they there all night; but at day break William Comyn, with a jolly ruffling crew, broke the doors and rushed into the church. Then might you see mailed coats gleaming amidst the shrines, archers mingling with monks, weeping and praying and threatening their invaders with heaven's vengeance, the whole Church, like a stormy sea, in tumult and uproar. Yet did they though scantly keep their hands off the monks; but when they had felled one of them with a stone, they left a guard of soldiers and archers in the Church, and drew off, dancing with joy, to light their fires and cook their meat, using for frankincense the savour of their roasted flesh, and for the song of the choristers the mad shouts of reckless wasters with the braying and bellowing of horns'. Early in 1144 the Earl of Northumberland and the Bishop joined forces in order to conclude the dispute. They advanced on Gilesgate to find that Cumin's men had fired not only that suburb but also Elvet before withdrawing.

The settlement and hospital were rebuilt shortly after, for the hospital was operating again by 1172. In 1180 Bishop Hugh of Le Puiset rebuilt the church, and moved the hospital to the foot of the hill. He confirmed the previous endowment, added the vill of Clifton and, by a separate charter, granted free burgage to Kepier Hospital and 'to all their men to whom they have granted liberty in the suburb of St Giles'. Gilesgate has scarcely changed since then, being two rows of properties facing one another across a green widening to the north-east. That was blocked by a row of houses, punctuated at one end by the road which branches to Sunderland and Sherburn House. The Church, set back from the frontage, occupied the centre of the south side. The boundary between the City and Gilesgate is still marked by a narrow lane athwart the ridge and nearer the City than St Giles Church. This boundary, between St Giles and St Nicholas parishes, was marked by a cross. There was a leaden cross there as early as 1454 which remained well into the seventeenth century; in 1660 some repairs were carried out but, a century later, only the pedestal remained. The long string of houses on the road from the City to Gilesgate has always been there, serving the agricultural borough, and at one time also pilgrims and other travellers entering the City from the north-east.

As the result of high-handed action by Bishop Hugh of Le Puiset, a second settlement came into being east of the peninsula. The first was the village of Elvet, centred on St Oswald's Church, while the second was created when Bishop Hugh, without authority or licence, took some of the Priory lands of Elvet into his own hands and built thereon a borough known as Elvethaugh. It was intended to hold forty merchants' houses. He did this in about 1180 and at the same time built Elvet Bridge, connecting the borough directly to the Market Place. This was useful since there was no market in Elvet (nor in Gilesgate). Bishop Hugh repented of this unlawful action (to which the Prior and Convent had properly objected) and in 1195 returned the borough to its rightful owners.

Known today as Old Elvet, it was laid out as two rows of houses facing one another across a broad street, a plan still clearly recognisable. The boundary between the borough and Elvet was on the line of a lane then known as Rotten Row, but more recently as Court Lane.

The two settlements, connected by the road leading to Bishop Hugh's bridge, were joined in the course of the late thirteenth or early fourteenth centuries by houses built on its line. The properties on the west side of the road were subject to periodic inundation. There was extensive flood damage in the late thirteenth or early fourteenth centuries and again in the mid-fourteenth century. A wall to contain the river was build in the later fourteenth century. Colonisation of the road, less persistent from the Elvet than the Borough end, eventually resulted in the fusion of the two settlements by the end of the fourteenth century. The Priory's village of Elvet prospered then for, not only did it extend northwards to meet the borough, but it spread southwards down the line of Hallgarth and Church Streets. Hallgarth Street derives its name from the Priory's manor and the tithe barn which still survives as part of the Prison Officers' Club. Adjacent agricultural buildings have in recent years been cleared to make way for prison extensions. By the mid-fourteenth century the Priory's officers were treating Elvet and the Borough as a single settlement of borough status.

The west bank of the Wear at Framwellgate Bridge, probably always the most important approach to the peninsula, held the borough of Crossgate (or the Old Borough) and Framwellgate. The Priory settlement there was elevated to borough status at some point in the twelfth century, and received the appellation of Old Borough when its second borough at Elvethaugh was created in 1180. Access to the southern end from the peninsula was afforded by the river crossing at the Water Gate in the South Bailey. The Priory had an orchard and fishponds behind the west side of South Street. The borough courts were held in the Tolbooth at the north end of Crossgate. There was also a prison in South Street. The court was concerned with debt collecting and general administration. A particular concern was animals (especially pigs) running loose and the accumulation of household refuse and manure where it had been deposited in the streets.

The north boundary of the borough was the stream draining Flass Bog, called the Millburn, by virtue of its use by the Bishop's mill at its confluence with the Wear. This mill was granted to Kepier Hospital in 1112, and suggests a date by which Framwellgate had been settled by the Bishop's tenants. Its ultimate successor was the Clock Mill, which survived well into the nineteenth century.

The findings of recent excavation in the middle reaches of Framwellgate suggest that the line of the road was not fixed until the thirteenth century, since a series of compressed occupation layers belonging to the twelfth century advanced up the slope towards the present street frontage, first used by a stone house built in the thirteenth century. From the beginning, the occupants were moderately wealthy, since they used imported pottery from Stamford and Germany.

None of the boroughs experienced self-government until the mid-sixteenth century. From the foundation until then, Kepier Hospital administered Gilesgate, the Priory, through its bailifs, Old Borough, Elvethaugh and Elvet. In the sixteenth century the ownership of Gilesgate passed to the secular owners of Kepier Hospital, the Bishop retained control of the City and Framwellgate while the Dean and Chapter, successors to the Prior and Convent, administered Elvet and Crossgate. This was only changed when the Municipal Borough was created by Act of Parliament in 1835.

In 1565 Bishop James Pilkington granted a charter of incorporation to the burgesses of Durham City and Framwellgate, the City to be administered by an Alderman and twelve burgesses elected annually. However, the Bishop retained the powers of veto on appointments and decisions made by the body corporate. This charter was replaced by a less restrictive one by Bishop Toby Matthew in 1602, which ordained that there should be a Mayor, twelve Aldermen and twenty four burgesses, two from each of the craft guilds, forming together the Common Council. It received Royal confirmation in 1605. Hutchinson, in patriotic mood, adds the rider . . . 'though it is apprehended, the bishop was competent to make his charter without the aid of the crown, and therefore this badge of honour, after the gilding of its dignity was removed, was no better than a scab on the constitution and privileges of the palatinate'.

Bishop Crewe granted a new charter in 1684 but, because of a supposed error in the procedure accompanying the surrender of the old charter, that of 1602 remained in force until 1751. In 1728 the Corporation passed a by-law to the effect that freemen of the City could only be drawn from those who had served their time as apprentices in one or other guilds. The legality of this decision they tested in 1757, when Robert Green, who satisfied none of these requirements, was elected a burgess. The by-law of 1728 was found by the courts to be binding.

The Corporation repealed the 1728 by-law in 1761 and soon after, 264 people who had no entitlement to franchise under the recently repealed by-law, were admitted freemen. The sole purpose of this was to ensure the election of Major Ralph Gowland as MP for Durham City and, since 215 of the new franchisees supported him, he won. Gowland's election was contested in the House of Commons by Major-General John Lambton, who had the highest number of votes under the old laws of the Corporation. The House found in his favour and he was duly elected in May 1762. The Bishop's Visitation Return of 1792 for Pittington Parish casts some light on this highly dubious event. 'Major Gowland had a Good Estate in this Parish on which the Presbyterians had £700 (called their Fund) for their Minister's Salary; this I understand the major made free with & spent in a contested election for the City of Durham . . .' As might be expected, the Presbyterians had all returned to the fold by 1792.

At the elections to the Common Council in 1766 irregularities occurred. These were tested in the courts and the qualifications of the Mayor and four Aldermen were found wanting. A further Alderman resigned and two died, leaving the number of Aldermen below that required for election of either Mayor or further Aldermen. Since the Mayor and Aldermen elected the Common Council, the Corporation ceased to exist. Bishop Egerton revived the Corporation in 1780 by granting a new charter. Some fifty years later, the divided jurisdiction of a single City, for it had effectively become so by then, was unified through the Municipal Corporations Act of 1835, when the Corporation was reformed and the franchise enlarged to the whole of the complex that is Durham. The present District Council is the modern descendant of that reformed organisation, and reflects a further enlargement of the franchise since 1835.

Bishop Hugh of le Puiset's Charter to the Burgesses of Durham in 1179
and its confirmation by Pope Alexander III.

69

LEFT: Silver seal of the Corporation, given by Matthew Pattison in 1606.
RIGHT: No 2, North Bailey; 17th century rubbish tip outside the Castle
Wall, both of which have been truncated by an early 18th century house.
(PAGC) BELOW: The Castle dominates the City physically and was also
the seat of the Bishops' power over the City.

ABOVE: The Bishop's administrative buildings on Palace Green: Diocesan Registry (1820) replacing the former Court House, Bishop Cosin's Library and the Exchequer: Joseph Bouet, 1824. (DC Add MS 95)
BELOW: Junction of Saddler Street and Elvet Bridge: Magdalen Steps mark the site of a building demolished by the Local Board of Health in c1860. (PAGC)

LEFT: Elvet Bridge. (PAGC) RIGHT: East end of Elvet Bridge showing the site of St Andrew's chantry chapel, 1883. BELOW: New Elvet, Hallgarth Street, Durham Prison and Whinney Hill School, pre-1950. (DC)

ABOVE: Gilesgate from halfway down Gilesgate Bank, 1923. (DUAD)
BELOW: Framwellgate in 1902. (AHR)

LEFT: Framwellgate and Milburngate in 1843, R. W. Billings. RIGHT: 18th century ice-house excavated on Framwellgate. (TW) BELOW: Paved backyard of a 13th-14th century stone-built house on Framwellgate with overlying 17th century drain and house. The wheel barrow covers a 19th century well. (PAGC)

Crafts, Coal and Carpets

The presence of a Market Place by 1040 reflects a community involved in trade. Given the relatively small areas of land available for growing produce, the market was the stomach of the town. People from neighbouring villages brought in surplus produce and exchanged it for manufactured goods. The excavations at 61-63 Saddler Street proved the manufacture and repair of shoes. Saddler Street was perhaps named because leather-workers were concentrated there. Fleshergate (Fleshewergate), that part of Saddler Street between Elvet Bridge and the Market Place, held the butchers. It was still their stronghold in the late 18th century, for William Hutchinson commented in 1787:
'We are led to lament that want of police in the city which should correct the brutal spectacle of slaughtering animals in the street; shocking to travellers, who instantly turn aside in disgust, and pass to other places, not only with prejudice of mind against the whole place, but with censure on its inhabitants'.

The more noisome trades such as tanning were kept at a distance. Excavation in Framwellgate has produced cattle horn-cores in sufficient numbers to suggest that tanning took place there throughout the medieval period, and certainly into the mid-seventeenth century. Indeed, the seventeenth century dump of horn-cores contained the earliest evidence so far for long-horned cattle in North East England, and a broken ivory die for stamping hides with the tanner's mark before selling. More recently the same area was occupied by Messrs Blagdon, who continued the tradition of leatherworking.

Butchery was not entirely restricted to Fleshergate, for an excavation has shown that butchers were dumping their rubbish below Back Silver Street in the fifteenth and sixteenth centuries. This Back Lane area was unsuitable for dwellings because of its steep slope. A drying kiln was built in the mid-thirteenth century, cutting into rubbish which had been accumulating on the slope since the late eleventh or early twelfth centuries. Later that century it was demolished. For the better part of three centuries, rubbish — including butchers' waste — was dumped down the slope to the river. An unidentified circular brick-built structure with a pantiled roof and a central roof support was built in the early seventeenth century. Further dumping occurred during the later seventeenth and eighteenth centuries until a clay tobacco pipe maker worked in the area. The maker is believed to have been William Dryden, working in Silver Street between 1827 and 1834.

In the fourteenth century, some Durham merchants make their appearance. John and William de Cotes carried wool and hides to the continent and returned with fine cloths, spices and wine. Robert de Cokside (or Coxhide) bought corn and tanning bark (from the Bearpark estate) from Durham Priory in 1339, and supplied it with groceries and liveries. John de Cotes bought wool from the Priory in 1238 and supplied it with almonds, sugar, wax, cloth and wine between 1327 and 1329. By 1343 he had died and his son Thomas was claiming customs allowances of £164 at Kingston upon Hull. John had also had an allowance at Hartlepool of £300 in 1338. These seem to be the only substantial merchants then.

The tradesmen of Durham eventually organised themselves into trade guilds, protecting their own interests against outside traders and had their rules (or Ordinaries) confirmed by the Bishop from time to time. Only twelve guilds occur in the Borough charters of 1565 and 1602, though there were at least sixteen. The Borough charters refer solely to Durham City and Framwellgate, whereas the Common Council was drawn from the freemen of the trade guilds, who might be resident in any part of the group of boroughs.

Some of the trade guilds, when they first occur, are quite clearly amalgamated with others. The prime example is the Mercers (1393), Grocers (1345), Haberdashers (1467), Ironmongers (1464) and Salters (1394) whose Ordinary was confirmed in 1560. Other guilds are paired. The Skinners and Glovers were formed about 1507, though a skinner does occur in 1429 and they claim to have been incorporated in 1327. By 1699 the Skinners and Glovers had met on Skinner's Hill 'beyond the New Bridge', certainly for twenty-three years. The Carpenters and Joiners are said to have been formed in the time of Bishop Tunstall (1530-38), but their earliest records only go back to 1661. The Wrights may have been included in the Carpenters and Joiners for in 1430 there were several Wrights involved as security for the good behaviour of one of their number. This suggests a possible guild which has no surviving records at all in the fifteenth century. Certainly by 1661, the guild included carpenters, joiners, wheelwrights, sawyers and coopers. The Curriers and Chandlers were in existence by 1570. The Fullers and Feltmakers were originally described as Clothworkers and Walkers in a charter of 1565, when they had 45 members. Walkers occur as early as 1440 and presumably worked in the vicinity of Walkergate. In 1448 fifteen fullers were prohibited from employing any native of Scotland, which suggests that there was already a guild by that date. In 1636 they were granted a new charter by which the guild was known as the 'Cloath-workers, Walkers, Cloath-fullers, Cloath-dressers, Hatt-makers and Felt-makers'. The Saddlers and Upholsterers appear to have no extant charter confirming their Ordinary. A saddler occurs in 1596 and the earliest records of the guild start in 1628.

The Rough Masons, Wallers and Slaters are said to have had their Ordinary confirmed in 1594. In 1609, presumably when other trades were brought within the purview of the guild, the Ordinary was again confirmed by the Bishop and the name changed to Rough Masons, Wallers, Slaters, Pavois, Tylers and Plasterers. In 1638 a new charter was given by the Bishop since they now included the Free Masons and Bricklayers. The Ordinary of the Barbers, Waxmakers and Surgeons is dated 1468. Almost two centuries later, the Ropers and Stringers joined them and a new Ordinary was drawn up in 1655. The Smiths occur as a guild in the charter of 1565. The term seems to have been a wide one for, by 1730, the full title of the craft was 'Whitesmiths, Lorimers, Locksmiths, Cutlers and Blacksmiths'. The Bladesmiths and Cutlers were separate crafts from the mid-sixteenth century until the later seventeenth century, when it was decreed by the Bishop that the Cutlers and Bladesmiths should admit Blacksmiths and *vice versa*.

The Cordwainers' Ordinary is dated 1458, but it is clear that the craft existed a decade earlier, for in 1448 the Bishop ordered seventeen cordwainers not to employ a native of Scotland. Shoemakers, of course, occur much earlier, though in the archaeological rather than the documentary record.

In 1450 twenty-two Weavers and Websters signed the earliest Ordinary of their craft to come down to us. It includes a specific statement that 'Noe man of the crafte within the Citty shall take to prentes [apprentice] noe Scottesman nor noe Scottesswoman'. In 1468 there was a dispute between the woollen websters and challon websters concerning the texture of cloths. The matter was settled at an inquest before Richard Raket, Serjeant of the Borough, and a jury. It was decided by the jury that woollen websters had always made woollen cloths and linen cloths, plain linen, caresay, sack cloth and hair cloth and the challon websters had likewise made and woven coverings, tapestry work, say, worsted, motleys, twilled work and dyaper. The two crafts were to continue making these cloths and not those of the other craft. The fine for breaking the ruling was £5.

The Drapers and Taylors' Ordinary was confirmed by Bishop Tunstall in 1549. However, taylors occur in the records from at least 1421 and drapers from 1521, which suggests that there may have been a craft or crafts of that name in the fifteenth century. Concerned about maintaining their monopoly, they brought four people to the Chancery Court in 1705. The charges against them included not being freemen of the guild (even though one had served his time in the appropriate guild in Darlington) and making and selling cloth and clothes within the borough. Not only were they trading without qualification, but one of them and two of their wives were making and selling currently fashionable mantuas and petticoats for women. The case was argued hard on both sides, but the craft won in the end.

The Dyers and Listers (or Litsters) is a guild which has been defunct since 1811. There are few records and none earlier than 1780. However, litsters occur as early as 1430. The Ordinary of the Goldsmiths was confirmed by Bishop Tunstall in 1532 when the craft is described as the goldsmiths, plumbers, pewterers, potters, glaziers and painters. The potters probably had their kilns in the area south of the peninsula now known as Potters' Bank. A regrettably incomplete archaeological record suggests that there was a sixteenth century kiln used for making 'cistercian' ware, which was disturbed when the new block of St Mary's College was erected in 1962. There were goldsmiths on the peninsula from at least the twelfth century, since they were involved in striking coins at the mint just inside Owengate until the seventeenth century.

The Butchers' Ordinary is dated 1520 and rules that no freeman shall slaughter animals on Thursdays after 12 noon or on Sunday before 1 pm. Probably one of the best known of Durham's citizens is John Duck, a freeman of the guild. He came to Durham and was apprenticed to a butcher, probably John Heslop. While walking at the waterside he was surprised by a raven which dropped a gold coin at his feet. This he put to good use and rapidly rose in his trade (not without some purchases against both the guild's rules and the law). He was also able to speculate, purchase and invest in land and collieries. In 1680 he was elected Mayor and in the same year was admitted a freeman of the butchers' guild. Six years later, for political services rendered, he was created a baronet. He left two monuments. The first was his magnificent mansion, which stood at the top of Silver Street (the Bulls Head and more recently Lyons Café) until it was demolished in 1963. The other is in the floor of the nave of St Margaret's Church.

The Barkers and Tanners seem to have been established before 1547. Individuals occur in the records during the preceding century, so again the guild may have been formed earlier than the earliest record.

The purpose of the trade guilds or crafts was to control the recruitment, methods and standards of their freemen. They also acted as friendly societies, paying pensions, grants to distressed brethren, providing palls at funerals and saying masses for the souls of the departed. The Tanners, for example, paid 5s to the poor of the trade in Gilesgate in 1616. There were two wardens and two stewards, who were divided between Gilesgate and Framwellgate, which suggests that the freemen of the trade were mainly resident there.

At the regular quarterly and other meetings, when freemen of the tanners were called to answer for the error of their ways, a jury of twelve was elected. One of the commonest misdemeanours was buying hides 'contrary to our order'. The order, repeated from time to time, is that by consent of the whole occupation 'noe man shall buy any butchers hids in their shoppes or houses but in open markett on the markett day. Upon every offender soe offending to pay ten shilling to the Bushopp and ten shillings to the occupation'. That was in

1622. In 1629 the order had been changed so that hides could only be bought 'upon the skin hill', and the fine had been reduced to a total of 6s 8d. Ten years later the order prohibiting the purchase of hides away from the skin hill includes 'or buy of the butchers by any privatt contract . . .'.

Seemly behaviour of apprentices was a matter of concern in 1652 and the Tanners ordered that apprentices 'shall at all tymes hereafter demeyne & behave themselves decently and reverently towards every freeman of the said Society . . . ypon payne that the Master of such Apprentice who shall be Carelesse & Negligent in performance herof to forfeit to the Wardens & Searchers &c . . . 3s 4d'. The examples set by the freemen such as Ralph Taylor and Gregory Hutchinson, both fined 12d for 'undecent speaches' towards one another, can scarcely have helped matters.

Harvesting oak bark in the Dean and Chapter's estate at Bearpark in April and May each year seems to have been a communal activity. Each member collected and paid for his share of the bark and carted it home in sight of the wardens and searchers. In 1645 nine tanners paid a total of £66 13s 4d for the bark yet to be stripped. Having got it, they were not allowed to sell off any surplus, but had to share it with needy freemen. They were also forbidden to purchase bark from sources other than those agreed by the whole guild.

One of the functions of the trade guild was in controlling the number of apprentices (generally one to each freeman) who served for seven years (nine for a tanner), ensuring that his work was of a suitable standard and then enrolling him as a freeman of that particular guild for a fee providing he was 21 years old (24 for a tanner). The number of freemen varied from guild to guild, the tanners having about forty (44 in 1624, 39 in 1643 and 40 in 1678). It became increasingly common from the early years of the seventeenth century for locally eminent men to be elected honorary freemen. The earliest honorary tanner on record is George Clark, admitted on 1 October 1628 who 'doth faithfullie promise this dae that he will not at any tyme take any apprentice whereby the said trade and misterie of tanners may be preiudiced either by himselfe or any under color or pretence of his admittance'.

In 1436 the Bishop granted a licence to the Constable and Clerk of the borough of Durham with others 'to institute anew' the fraternity or guild of Corpus Christi. It was to consist both of men and women, and had powers to elect or remove the master or warden who had custody of the lands of the guild. The Bishop allowed the guild to acquire land yielding up to £10 per annum. This was the great civic guild which had a grand procession on the Thursday after Trinity Sunday. The procession started with the bailiff standing in the Tollbooth in the Market Place, and calling the craft guilds to bring their banners and lights out of St Nicholas church. Then came the Corpus Christi shrine 'all fynlye gilted . . . and on the hight of the sayd shrine was a foure squared Box all of christall, wherein was enclosed the holy sacrament of the aulter . . .'. It was brought forth by four priests who carried it in procession to Palace Green, being preceded by processions from all the other churches in Durham. On Palace Green the shrine stopped at Windy Gap and the banners and lights (or torches) of the craft guilds formed an avenue between there and the north door of the church, the banners on the east side, and the torches on the west. The monks then brought out St Cuthbert's banner and two crosses and led the whole procession into the church, where St Cuthbert's banner was set in the choir, and the craft guild banners set around St Cuthbert's shrine. A service was said and the Te Deum sung. The whole procession was then reversed and the Corpus Christi shrine returned to St Nicholas Church, where it rested in the vestry for the coming year.

This will have been the opening event in a day when the town in all its parts celebrated its existence. There then followed the plays that 'of olde tymes longes to their craft' as the Barbers Ordinary of 1468 has it. Each craft had its own play representing a Bible story, which it presented in the town, perhaps in the Market Place.

After the Restoration the annual procession became more subdued, for the Corpus Christi shrine had been smashed by Dean Horne and Saint Cuthbert's banner burnt by Dean Whittingham's wife not long after (perhaps testing the legend that it was fireproof). In 1660 the day was moved to Restoration Day (29 May) and a sermon in St Nicholas Church substituted for the grand procession. Even in the eighteenth century the banners graciously decorated the church, but now only exist as a series of paintings.

The nature of the craft guilds changed during the seventeenth century for, through the Common Council, they became increasingly involved in politics. In 1617 they presented a petition to King James when he visited Durham, asking for Parliamentary representation. Bishop James and his successors strenuously opposed the move for, if granted, it would have eroded the Bishop's power and allowed the burgesses direct access to the King through Parliament. During the interregnum the City was represented in Parliament, but this was lost at the Restoration. Eventually, on 27 March 1678, 838 freemen of the town voted for their two MPs, Sir Ralph Coles and John Parkhurst. While the guilds continued to function as before, the increasing number of honorary freemen diluted the trade interest in favour of politics. The Parliamentary by-election of 1761 was merely on instance of this. The guilds lost all direct involvement in politics as a result of the widening of the franchise under the Reform Act of 1832 and the Municipal Corporations Act of 1835. Thereafter their function was almost entirely honorific.

Laurels for industrial activity crown County rather than City. The City, however, had more than a passing interest in coal. Both the Bishop and the Dean and Chapter from earliest times had considerable interests in these ventures, gaining substantial revenues thereby. Several other residents of the City risked fortunes for the profits that accompanied the successful winning of coal. In the immediate area of the City, mines were sunk on Elvet, Gilesgate and Framwellgate Moors. The Enclosure Award of Elvet Moor in 1772 refers to some mines. The earliest known with any certainty is the Elvet landsale colliery which occurs in 1815 and was probably abandoned in 1816. A new Elvet Colliery started in 1828 with greater succcess and continued to produce coal for some years. A mine was started at Kepier Grange in 1818 and flourished for a time. It was given a new lease of life when the railway came in 1842. Despite attempts to find new coal, the mine was abandoned in the 1880s. There were exploratory borings on Framwellgate Moor in 1815 but no pit was started until 1838. In that year the Northern Coal Mining Company sank a pit which was completed in 1841. There was a great scramble for shares in this promising investment. Unfortunately, production was considerably less than anticipated and in the mid-1840s the company collapsed, having lost all its subscribed capital of £500,000 and rather more besides. The Marquess of Londonderry then successfully worked the Royalty, sinking new pits in the 1860s (Durham Main) and Aykley Heads in the 1880s. In 1898 there was a tramway (later converted to an aerial ropeway) direct from the Durham Main Pit to the Gas Works in Framwellgate. The mine was abandoned in 1922 and finally closed three years later.

Coke ovens and brickworks are frequently part of collieries. At Framwellgate Moor there were 237 beehive coke ovens in 1859. In 1895 there were anything from 98 to 205 ovens working at any one time. This mine also had a brickworks, and there was another near Crook Hall which had started as part of a short-lived Sidegate Pit in the early 19th century. It stopped work in 1968 when it threatened to undermine the main line railway. The settlements at Framwellgate Moor, Pity Me, Carrville and Belmont owe their existence to these various collieries, for they were built to house the men, women and children who worked in and around them.

The financing of the pits came from a variety of sources, rents or subscriptions by share holders, and ultimately from banks. Messrs Backhouse & Co, a Darlington bank founded in

1772, had an agent in Durham from as early as 1778 — Benjamin Dunn — who described himself in 1790 as mercer, draper and banker. At one point he was in partnership with a Mr Oyston. Another mercer, draper and banker, William Shields, was operating in 1790. Shortly after, he became a partner in another local bank (Richardson and Mowbray) which failed in 1815. The bank had advanced too much to Easterby, Hall & Co, which worked lead mines in Arkendale and Derwent. This firm collapsed in 1815 owing substantial debts, not the least being £170,000 to Richardson and Mowbray. A banking partnership of Mills, Robinson, Hopper, Pearson, and Chipchase, apparently referred to as The Durham Bank was formed shortly before 1787. It successfully overcame runs on its assets in 1793 and 1797. In 1802 the partnership was dissolved and the business transferred to Richardson and Mowbray. In 1856 there were two banks in Durham: Backhouse's agent, J. W. Barnes and the Northumberland and District Bank. The latter, founded in 1836, crashed in 1857 with substantial liabilities.

Durham mustard was famed in the eighteenth and nineteenth centuries. This particularly pungent blend seems to have been developed in the 1720s, and continued in production well into the nineteenth century, when it was overwhelmed by the availability of a cheaper product. One of the manufacturers was the printer and stationer William Aynsley, whose premises are now occupied by Martins (until recently House of Andrews) in Saddler Street.

In the early seventeenth century the City Corporation had unsuccessfully established a woollen factory in the New Place by St Nicholas Church, as a means of employing indigent poor. In 1689 Thomas Craddock bequeathed £500 to build a house and workhouses for a master and workmen, so that another woollen factory could be established, again for the benefit of the poor. In spite of help lent by the charity, Messrs Startforth and Cooper, running the factory on the lines of Abrose Crowley's ironworks at Whickham, failed to make it pay. The County Justices advertised in 1814 that they were willing to advance £400 to anyone willing to re-establish the concern, who was able to give good securities. Gilbert Henderson, a Merrington weaver, obtained the loan. He took over Startforth and Cooper's premises and built up a sound business, which developed rapidly. He managed it single-handed until his eldest son, John, had completed his schooling. Then John, and later another son, William (who withdrew from the firm in the early 1870s), assisted and eventually took over the business. John Henderson became increasingly involved in local politics and in 1864 was one of a pair of Liberal MPs returned for the City. By that time George Henderson, one of his sons, was running the factory. In 1874 John Henderson MP, coal owner and carpet manufacturer, was described as 'a man of business who speaks like a ledger. His speeches are a plain unvarnished account of facts rendered luminous by a shrewd and practical common sense'.

On 25 October 1860 Messrs Henderson & Company wrote to the Local Board of Health complaining 'that the Quay Wall by the Waterside near the Market Place Mill which was partly rebuilt in Spring of last year remains yet unfinished' and also that the pavements in the neighbourhood were in a bad condition. The Board inspected the road immediately and, at its meeting on 2 November, received the report that 'the present state of the roadway is principally caused by Messrs Henderson having constructed a flue and laid down steam pipes from the old Factory in the Back Lane under the roadway to the new factory'. Hendersons had done this without permission and the Board recommended that Hendersons repair the roadway at their own expense.

By this time Durham carpets had achieved international fame. In 1903 the goodwill of the Henderson carpet factory was sold to Messrs Crossley of Halifax. Part of the building was let to Hugh MacKay, buyer and manager of Henderson's. He started with 11 Brussels looms and 20 weavers (a far cry from the five hundred employed in 1874). Within a few years the business was paying its way, but it did not start to prosper until after the 1929 North East Coast

Exhibition, since when it has never looked back. In 1969 a disastrous fire destroyed some of the buildings, but production was in hand again within nine days. In 1970 the firm moved to its present location in Dragonville.

Almost synonymous with coal mines is the Durham Miners Association. The history of its predecessors in the first half of the nineteenth century is not a happy one. Associations were established in 1809 and, under Tommy Hebburn, a Northumberland and Durham union was formed in 1830. It struck in 1831 for shorter working hours and the abolition of the Tommy shop. The union won in 1832, achieving a reduction of working hours from 17 to 12 per day, but the coal owners would not re-employ union men. This led to further strikes and to violence and it was this that effectively ended the union, whose members were forced to revert to pre-union conditions. A decade later, the union was reformed and joined a national association. In 1844, under the leadership of Martin Jude, the miners struck for 18 weeks with the intention of resolving a series of grievances. The coal owners evicted striking miners and their families and kept the mines woking with imported and blackleg labour. They also got the workhouse closed against the miners. The prime mover among the coal owners was the Marquess of Londonderry, who earned himself no little opprobrium in local and national press. Nevertheless, his action broke the strike and, effectively, the union.

Another Northumberland and Durham Miners' Association was formed in 1863, but the Durham men acted in a series of unsuccessful strikes before the union was strong enough. A major setback was strike action at Willington, where the coal owners included Joseph Love, prominent in the Methodist New Connexion. The men struck because coal was measured by volume and not by weight. Love immediately evicted the miners and their families from Sunnybrow, Willington, Brancepeth and Oakenshaw. He got blackleg and imported labour to work the mines and this broke the strike. In 1865 Northumberland seceded from the joint union and the Durham side withered away. In 1869, however, a union was desparately needed, as there weree too many men for the owners to employ, the price of coal had dropped, and the owners were offering wages reduced by 15-20%. The miners found that they could not live on these wages and struck. This led to a union of delegates from a number of collieries, who appointed John Richardson their agent and co-ordinator. On 20 November of that year, the Durham Miners' Assocation was formed at a meeting in the Market Hotel, Durham. John Richardson was the agent and secretary. By the second half of 1870, the Association had established a central fund and had organised a means of settling disputes through a central Board. Negotiation and arbitration procedures were early established and these continued to be the basis for discussions with coal owners into this century.

In August 1871 the miners held a meeting in Wharton Park in Durham City with the intention of increasing membership. The meeting included band and sports competitions. This was the very first of the Durham Miners' Associations galas, at which two thousand people paid for admission. The gala has since become not just a symbol of solidarity of the miners but also a significant event in national politics.

In 1875 Miners' Hall was built on the site of Monks Buildings in North Road. Statues of four of the leaders were placed in front of the first floor windows: Alexander MacDonald, William Crawford, W. H. Patterson and John Forman. A new Durham Miners' Hall was opened on the Redhills on 23 October 1915 and the statues from the old hall were removed to stand on pedestals near the entrance. While the Miners' Association was principally concerned with wages and working conditions in the mines, it also took an active interest in the welfare of its members through its Central Fund, being involved in establishing the Aged Miners Homes.

The Durham Chamber of Trade was formed in 1913 and grew rapidly. In about 1926 there were some 200 members, but in the following three years seventy members were lost. The numbers climbed again slowly from the late 1930s to reach about 180 in 1956. Since then membership has been almost halved. This reflects the fluctuating fortunes of the multitude of retail and wholesale trades in the town during this century. Between the wars the depression was a major influence on Chamber. Since the last War, the decline has been the result of local family firms closing, replaced by others whose main office is not in Durham.

In the early 1960s the Chamber organised and mobilised opposition to the redevelopment schemes that have since been carried out in the City centre. In the mid-1960s, concerned about the image of Durham, the Chamber asked the City Council to 'eliminate all derelict buildings within the City at the earliest opportunity'.

Members of the Chamber of Trade included men like Harry Murdoch, Mayor in 1929-30, who had a chain of draper's shops know as Murdoch's Emporia, one of which was in Silver Street. Mr J. L. Myres, President of the Chamber of Trade in 1956-7, is the fourth generation of his family to trade in the worsted and yarn business. The Myres firm started in 1820. By 1846 George Myres occurs at 40 Framwellgate as a worsted dealer. Eight years later there was a shop at 14 Silver Street, replaced by two premises, 20 Market Place and 76 North Road by 1889. The North Road premises were used for spinning and dying wool. It was this wool that started the brand name 'Dunelm'. More recently the wool has been prepared in Darlington and now Bradford. The brand name, however, continues, as does the firm, into its fifth generation.

Gordon McIntyre, President of the Chamber of Trade in 1955-6, was the proprietor of J. & G. Archibalds, the interests of which his father William had bought in 1924. John and George Archibald had taken over Mr Tomlinson's prosperous iron and steel business, which he had started in North Road in 1840 and then moved up to the Goods Station in Gilesgate in 1884. After 1926, when the iron and steel trade suffered badly, Archibald's developed their present builder's merchanting business. In 1938 St Giles Parish Hall, which has now succumbed to the new road leading down to Elvet Bridge, was converted to a showroom. Eighteen years later the present showroom in North Road was built and opened.

In 1910 H. J. Fentiman was using a building, previously part of the Hallgarth Farm Complex in New Elvet, for the production of aerated water. By 1930 A. Broughton was using the premises, since a licence to store up to 500 gallons of petrol was issued that year. It was only in 1937 that the building was registered under the Factory and Workshop Act, 1901, for the purposes of botanical brewing (ginger beer) and mineral water manufacture. The firm of Fentiman's Direct Supply Company ceased to trade in 1974 and the premises were demolished in 1976. The main manufacturer of mineral water in Durham throughout this century has always been Wood and Watson in Gilesgate.

Copies of four of the Guilds' coats of Arms made in 1784-5 when they were still hanging in St Nicholas Church. They are now in the Guildhall.
(DCC)

BUTCHERS

WEAVERS

SKINNERS & GLOVERS

DRAPERS and TAILORS

The Auntient solemnytie of *festession* vpo *corpus xristi*
day *w*th in *y* *e* church and citie of Durham /
before *y* *e* suppressio of *y* *e* said abbey Churche ~

There was a goodly *processio* vpo *y* *e* place quene *on*
thursday after Trinitie sonndaye in *y* *e* Honor of *corp*
Christi said *y* *e* *w*th was a pryncipall feast at that
tyme The baley of *y* *e* towne did all *y* *e* vnyparable
that was inhabitors w*th* in *y* *e* towne ody *vnyvitio*
in his degree to bringe forthe ther Bans w*th* All ther
lightes apptynings to ther *so all* Bands c to
repaire to *y* *e* abbey church done ody banner to
stand a rowe in his degree from *y* *e* abbey church
done to wyndshole yett on *y* *e* weste *of* *y* *e* way
did all *y* *e* Bands stand, and on *y* *e* easte shyde of
y *e* way dyd all *y* *e* Torges stand apptynings to *y* *e*
sayd Banners :/

ABOVE: Lewin's hauliers delivering bricks and sand to the Castle
during its restoration, 1929. (DUAD) BELOW: A 16th century account
of the Corpus Christi procession. (DC MS C.III.23)

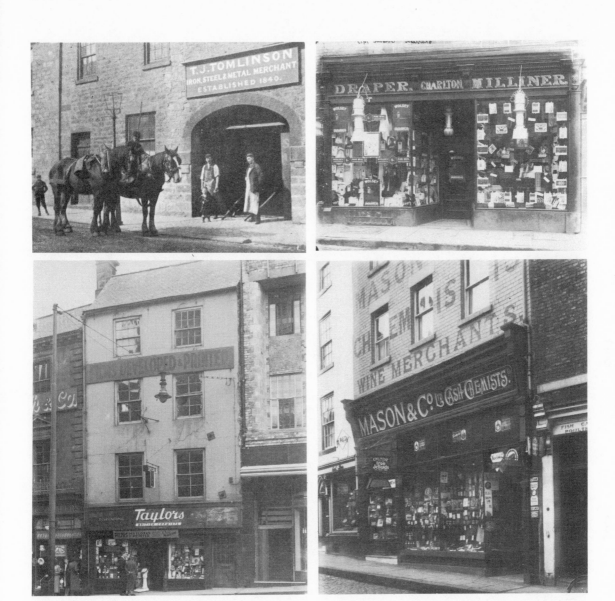

ABOVE LEFT: T. J. Tomlinson's establishment in North Road. (JGA)
RIGHT: Charlton's, Draper and Milliner, 1913. (DUAD) BELOW
LEFT: Taylor's the chemist, Market Place, 1938. (DUAD) RIGHT:
Masons, Chemists and Wine Merchants, Market Place, 1938. (DUAD)

OPPOSITE LEFT: The Market Hotel, Market Place (where the Durham Miners Association was formed in 1871), 1919. (DUAD) CENTRE: J. L. Myers' labels for wool. (PAGC) RIGHT: Middleton's Cocoa Rooms in the Market Place (where W. H. Smith is now) in 1901, with the proprietor and his son standing in the doorway. (ARM) BELOW: Drawing of Durham showing on the east bank of the Wear (with two tall chimneys) Henderson's Carpet Factory as it was in 1883. ABOVE LEFT: Archibald's transport waiting at the Goods Station Depot, Gilesgate 1940. (JGA) RIGHT: Loading pipes and cement there. (JGA) CENTRE LEFT: Despatch depot of MacKays Carpet Factory, 1929. (HM) RIGHT: their first Axminster loom, 1935; (HM) BELOW LEFT: weaving shed No 2, 1929, (HM) and RIGHT: after the 1970 fire. (HM)

ABOVE: St Oswald's church, 1824; Joseph Bouet. BELOW: St Giles church, 1824; Joseph Bouet. (Both DC Add MS 95)

Let Us All Pray

Churches and chapels are mirrors of the corporate pride and aspirations of those who worship in them, whether they be grand twelfth century parish churches or humble, late nineteenth century Nonconformist chapels. The medieval churches in Durham reflect the separate identities of the several communities that constitute Durham. St Oswald, tall, airy and imposing; St Margaret, small, dark and intimate fall at either end of the spectrum. Between them lies St Giles, the two St Marys — both garrison churches — and St Nicholas, though 150 years ago St Nicholas might have taken the place of St Oswald. St Oswald is the only one of these churches to have had a pre-Norman predecessor, though whether this took the form of a church or a preaching cross is not known.

All of the other churches were erected in the first half of the twelfth century in response to settlement innovation. St Margaret was created as a chapel of ease within St Oswald's Parish to serve what became — for a short time at least — the most important settlement in the parish, when the borough of Crossgate was formed by the Priory. St Nicholas was created when the town of Durham was moved down onto the lower plateau in about 1100. St Giles was built initially as part of a hospital but, when that was refunded in the later twelfth century, the church became separated and St Giles became the parish church to serve that anomaly, the agricultural borough of Gilesgate. To mark this event the chancel was built anew. The churches of St Mary-le-Bow and St Mary-the-Less were both built in response to the need for churches to serve the Castle garrison quartered in the outer bailey. In consequence, both are relatively small. St Oswald's Church is the largest and grandest of the medieval churches that survive. It served a large parish, which may be equated with a pre-Norman estate within which, in the late twelfth century, was erected the borough of Elvethaugh. At the same time, the north and south aisles were added to the church, presumably to cope with the increase in the number of parishioners.

The subsequent history of these churches reflects that of the individual settlements which they served. St Giles saw little increase in size apart from the addition of a western tower in the early thirteenth century which was either completed or rebuilt as part of the general repair work needed on the church in the early fifteenth century, for which Bishop Langley granted an indulgence of forty days in 1414. Today only the tower, chancel and north wall survive within a predominantly nineteenth century church. St Oswald's Church saw little alteration until the early fifteenth century, when it was lengthened and a tower built. At the same time the nave and aisles were re-roofed. The clerestorey, which was embattled, was added as part of this major improvement. The vicar of the time, William Catten (1411-1414) was commemorated on the central boss: *Orate p.W. Catten vicr.* Unfortunately much of this was lost when the church suffered from the effects of Elvet Colliery's underground workings. The aisle walls and chancel were completely rebuilt, the clerestorey windows replaced, the magnificent parapet removed and the old roof completely destroyed. The fifteenth century choir stalls survived until destroyed by a fire in March 1984. The steps in the tower are re-used grave slabs.

By the beginning of the thirteenth century, St Margaret's Chapel in Crossgate consisted of a chancel, nave and north and south aisles. A chantry chapel to the Blessed Virgin had been founded by the end of the century and endowed with rents from various properties, principally in Framwellgate and the Old Borough. In 1343 Bishop Richard de Bury granted an Indulgence of forty days to all who contributed to the building of the south aisle.

The chapel was used for baptisms in the early fourteenth century, for in 1343 the Prior and Convent ordered the removal of the font. Later that year the Bishop ordered the font to be replaced and, at the same time, told the parishioners that they had no right to the sacraments in the chapel. Almost immediately afterwards, the Prior and Convent allowed the people of the Old Borough to be married in the chapel, to be baptised and for women to be churched. Eventually, in 1431 the parishioners sought, and were granted, permission to bury their dead because the mother church, St Oswald's, was inconveniently distant. This long-drawn-out process reflects the desires of the people of Crossgate to have their own parish church. While St Margaret's achieved all the attributes of a parish church in this period, the incumbent was not called a rector until 1873. There were also long and unseemly wrangles between St Oswald's and St Margaret's in the sixteenth to nineteenth centuries over assessments for repairs, for St Oswald's would not contribute to St Margaret's costs but demanded a contribution from the people in St Margaret's 'parish'.

The church was substantially rebuilt in the course of the fifteenth century. Structural weaknesses almost certainly lay behind this work. The western tower of three stages was built, and the only work that was not repairing and making good a falling structure was the construction of the tower, and that can almost be ascribed to fashion, since St Giles and St Oswald had their towers put up in this century too.

It is unfortunate for us that St Nicholas Church was torn down and rebuilt in 1857-8, for it was this church alone that had all of Durham's civic pride poured into it from an early date. It was large, with a somewhat eccentric plan, probably arrived at over a period. The church was in existence by 1133. Only the north arcade of the early chancel survived to 1800. The rest was built in the fourteenth or fifteenth centuries. Perhaps the most unusual feature was the position of the tower, placed at the west end of a truncated south aisle and affording the main entrance. Within the church there were four chantries: St Mary (pre-1250), St James (1382), St John the Baptist and St John the Evangelist (1407) as well as a chantry to the Holy Trinity. Elsewhere in the parish there were three chantry chapels. St Thomas the Martyr, founded in the thirteenth century, was situated on the north side of Claypath near its junction with Gilesgate parish. The other two chantry chapels were on either end of Elvet Bridge. That of St Andrew on the Elvet end of the bridge, was founded between 1274 and 1283, while that of St James, at the other end of the bridge, was in existence by 1393. The religious guilds, of which there were three in St Nicholas (Our Lady, St Nicholas and Corpus Christi) were the poor man's chantry chapel, since their members would pray for the souls of the departed and also help pay for their burial. It is quite clear that St Nicholas was the wealthiest of the Durham churches, almost certainly because of its position in the most important part of the town. This seems to have been recognised by Bishop Neville who appropriated the profitable rectory, together with its glebe at Old Durham, to Kepier Hospital in 1443. From that time until the Dissolution, St Nicholas was served by stipendiary priests belonging to the hospital.

The churchyards around all the churches are still visible except in the case of St Nicholas. Here it was divided into three parts. The largest section lay south of the church and faced onto the Market Place. A smaller section lay between the church and Back Lane on the north, while the third portion seems to have become separated. It lay west of the west end and had a vennel between it and the church. When corpses were carried to this portion of the churchyard, they went over the vennel on a drawbridge.

The southern portion of the churchyard was used by the leather market. In the seventeenth century, the vestry accounts include a sum paid for dressing the churchyard, also called clearing the midden. Occasionally we are told that the midden was cleared and tipped over the wall into the Back Lane. At least part of the midden will have come from within the church itself, since it seems not have been flagged and had rushes strewn on the floor once a year (around Whitsun or midsummer). The churchyard of St Giles, by contrast, was separated from the main street by the town's pinfold, a gap in the south row of Gilesgate that is still apparent today. On the southern side of the churchyard was a holy well, which was regularly maintained into the eighteenth century, when it had a cross put on top.

The vestry books provide a detailed acount of the repair and maintenance of the parish churches of Durham in the seventeenth and eighteenth centuries. Bells seem to have been a particular concern throughout the seventeenth century. Indeed, those of St Oswald were recast twice, in 1664-5 when four bells were recast by Sam Smith of Darlington. The second time was in 1694 when Christopher Hodgson was the founder. Recent excavation in the Blacksmith's Shop in the Cathedral precincts has revealed the remains of a bell mould which would have produced a bell identical to one of those still in St Oswald's tower. The sixteenth, seventeenth and eighteenth centuries saw relatively little repair work and that only when utterly necessary. The story in all the churches is one of basic maintenance and repair. The bells of St Oswald's, for example, were being constantly tinkered with from the first entry in the vestry book in 1580 until their recasting in 1664-5. Windows were regularly patched up, quarry by quarry rather than being completely made anew. The interiors were looked after rather better than the exteriors, for this was what people would see more closely than any other part of the church. The walls were whitewashed with reasonable regularity and the Lord's Prayer and Ten Commandments painted up on the walls for all to see. The floor of St Oswald's was flagged in 1630-1 at the same time as the interior was plastered and painted over and the exterior of the church rough cast. The floor in St Giles was flagged only in 1703, though the interior was maintained during the seventeenth century in much the same way as St Oswald's, with plaster and whitewash on which the 'sentences' were painted. St Nicholas was plastered, whitewashed and the Ten Commandments painted 'by order of the Lord Bishop' in 1684-5; he also required the floor to be flagged.

Despite all this maintenance work, some of the churches fell into a serious state of disrepair. St Mary-le-Bow partly collapsed in 1637 and was eventually rebuilt at the end of the century. It was restored yet again in 1873 and has in recent years been made redundant. Serving as the Durham City Trust's Heritage Centre, its roof has been repaired and recovered since 1976. St Mary-the-Less, apparently in need of repair from the late eighteenth century, was almost completely rebuilt in 1847. It seems likely that this work was a caprice on the part of Rev James Raine, the then rector, for the church had only shortly before been subjected to substantial repairs including underpinning the walls. It may be that Raine wanted to build his own purely 'Norman' church. It became St John's College chapel in 1919.

St Oswald was substantially rebuilt in 1834 and again in 1864 when a vestry was added to the chancel. St Giles was restored in 1828, the major calamity being Wyatt's almost complete removal of the chancel arch. St Margaret of Antioch, which seems to have been stuffed full of galleries in the late eighteenth century, was heavily restored in the course of the nineteenth century (1865, 1877, 1878-80).

All these restorations were necessary because of the state of the fabric. Windows, for example, had been replaced with sashes in the eighteenth century as an 'improvement'. Such was the case with St Nicholas Church, which also lost the eastern portion of its chancel to a road widening scheme. The church was quite clearly an encumbrance on the parish. Constant pointing of parts of the walls made them look as though they had been rendered. In the end the building was demolished and built anew on the lines of the earlier church. The design of the interior, however, was made more fitting for the current practices and expectations of the time. In 1981 the church again saw a major programme of repair work designed not only to make it more fit to worship in, but also to change its interior to fit the way the parishioners and incumbent saw the place of the Church in modern society. To day it is not just a church, but also a refuge from the Market Place with tea, coffee and a small craft shop. The market has indeed come into the church!

In the course of the seventeenth century, the registers of the parish churches in Durham refer to nonconformists (mostly Quakers and Presbyterians) buried or married in the parish. The story of Nonconformity goes back into the sixteenth century when a number of prebendaries of the Cathedral seem to have had puritan tendencies. They were not leaderless, for two Deans, Robert Horne and William Whittingham, together with Bishop Pilkington, represented a powerful puritanising force in the third quarter of that century. Whittingham, co-translator of the Geneva Bible and involved in the preparation of the Geneva Order Book while in exile during the reign of Queen Mary, was married to the sister of that arch reformer, John Calvin. The Chapter continued to have members with puritan tendencies into the seventeenth century. Indeed two of the early seventeenth century Bishops appointed men with such leanings to parishes. Bishop Morton appointed John Lapthorne, later described as 'a grave strict puritan' to serve in the north-west of County Durham. However, by the 1620s the Chapter was divided between those of puritan leanings and those who supported the up and coming William Laud, later Archbishop of Canterbury. Friction between the two parties reached its height when Peter Smart delivered some explosive sermons against the Laudian changes in 1628. They earned him a £500 fine which, since he refused to pay, was converted to prison, where he languished until 1640.

These men must have had some influence on their flocks, but no firm evidence has come down to us that either they or other incumbents were following their brethren elsewhere in the country in setting up conventicles, though no doubt some did. City and County were forcibly converted to Presbyterianism by Parliament in 1644 when parishioners were required to subscribe to the Solemn League and Covenant. The whole of the County was divided into Presbyteries, of which Durham City was one. It had four ministers: Anthony Lapthorne, Reuben Easthorpe, Henry Lever and Patrick Forbes. These are the first known nonconformist preachers in Durham City. In 1655 the Presbytery consisted of Robert Lever, John Thompson, Richard Frankland and Thomas Dixon.

The Presbyterian presence continued in Durham after the Restoration. In 1662 Thomas Dixon was 'turned out of his church [Kelloe] by one Pearson, whome Dr Cozens, then Bishop of Durham, had presented to the place . . . in a tumultuous manner'. He went to live in Durham and, in 1672 licensed his house in Claypath as a place of worship. After the Act of Toleration in 1688, it became a legal meeting house of the Presbyterian congregation. It was taken down in 1750 and a new chapel built which still survives, tucked down behind the frontage onto Claypath. This is one of the most attractive chapels built in Durham. While it was only accessible by a passage from the street, its size and scale are such as to suggest that the congregation was not trying to hide itself. Rather, it reflects a moderately wealthy group of people, proud of their faith and willing to proclaim it in bricks and mortar. One reason for their seeming affluence is that Robert Pleasaunce, their minister from 1662 to 1701, had bequeathed all his lands and collieries to Ralph Gowland, solicitor, of Durham City with the private direction that the interest from one sixth of Bitchburn Colliery be directed in equal parts to the support of the presbyterian ministers of Durham, Stockton and Sunderland. In his register, Mr Thompson of the Stockton church noted that Ralph Gowland, senior, died on 29 March 1728. 'He was renowned for his fair practice as an atorney at law. He was ready to engage in the cause of the poor when opprest. He was a geat friend to Dissenting Protestants, especially at Durham, the place of his abode. He was much confided in for his prudence and faithfulness: e.g. by the late Reverend Mr Pleasance, in his last will; and hath alwaies been thought to be true to that trust, by them that were concerned in it. The Lord Grant that his successor in that trust may follow his example therein'. The share of the colliery was sold in 1759 for £1,000 by Ralph Gowland, grandson of the executor. The interest was paid by him, somewhat irregularly until 1775. It is quite clear that it was this fund that Gowland misused in his attempt to be elected MP for Durham City in 1761. The members of the church dwindled until there were so few that they joined the Congregational Church of Framwellgate in 1804.

That church had been formed in 1778, when thirteen members had subscribed to sixteen Articles of Faith. From 1804, when they were joined by the Presbyterians, until 1820 there were two chapels with services at each on every Sunday despite a steady fall in numbers. Between 1820 and 1860, energetic work by the minister resulted in a dramatic increase. This was so great that in 1860 the Claypath Chapel was enlarged to hold 500 people. In the same year the Framwellgate Chapel was converted to a Sunday School and was later sold. The church continued to prosper and, in 1885, the houses between the 1750 chapel and Claypath were torn down and the present stone edifice erected. The old brick chapel was converted to Sunday School uses.

The Presbyterians (Scottish) came into Durham in 1872 and established a congregation which built its church at Waddington Street within the year. Recently Presbyterian and Congregational congregations in Durham have again united, this time to form the United Reformed Church.

A Quaker Meeting had been established in Durham as early as 1657. The meetings took place in John Heighington's house on Claypath. Funds were raised for a Meeting House in 1679, which was built and enlarged in 1693. It had a burial ground attached. The meeting was discontinued in 1859 and the Meeting House sold in 1873. After a false start in the 1930s, the Friends re-established a meeting in Durham in 1948.

A Wesleyan Methodist Society was formed in Durham in about 1743. It was not until 1770 that it converted a building in Rotten Row, Old Elvet, for use as a chapel. Membership grew in fits and starts until a new chapel was needed and built behind part of the County Hotel in 1808. This chapel was hardly distinguishable from a domestic house. It was rebuilt on Old Elvet at the beginning of this century in formal 'church' style, much as the Congregational and Presbyterian chapels had been at the end of the preceding century. It was opened in 1903. There were several other Wesleyan Methodist Societies with chapels in Durham: that at Gilesgate was established in 1865 and built its present chapel in 1869. A society was established at Dragonville some time before 1873, in which year it built a small chapel. In 1888 a schoolroom was added. Eventually the Society closed and joined the Gilesgate Society. That at Carrville was established in 1835, in which year it built its first chapel. Larger premises were erected in 1881, the former chapel sold for use as a concert hall. In 1932 the Society was amalgamated with the Primitive Methodist Society. At Framwellgate Moor there was a series of temporary meeting houses from 1827 until a chapel was built in 1896. In 1904 the Society moved to Pity Me, where the new chapel was of corrugated iron, later clad in brick. The Society closed in 1940.

The Primitive Methodist Society established a number of chapels in Durham City, chief of which was that built originally in Back Silver Street in 1825, which moved to a grand chapel, called the Jubilee Chapel in North Road in 1862. In the 1960s this Society merged with the Methodist New Connexion/United Methodist Society in North Road and sold the old chapel. Other Primitive Methodist chapels were situated at Belmont, where the Society was formed in 1835 and closed later that century. The Gilesgate Moor Society built a chapel in 1838 which was sold in 1947, three years after the Society had closed. At Carrville the Society first met in 1838 at 40 High Street. The year after, it built a chapel which ultimately proved inadequate and was replaced in 1869 by the present one, recently refurbished by the members. On Framwellgate Moor a society was established in 1838 with a small membership. In 1870 the Society bought two cottages and joined them together to form a chapel. The Society closed and the chapel was sold in its centenary year of 1938. Early this century a society was formed in Neville's Cross. It erected a corrugated iron chapel which was rendered with cement in the 1930s. The Society closed in 1981.

The Methodist New Connexion, which became a member of the United Methodist Church after 1907, had a society in Old Elvet which was established in 1828. It first met in 33 Old Elvet and later in the upper part of 15 Old Elvet. The foundation stones of the Bethel Chapel in North Road were laid in 1853 and the building opened for worship in 1854. In the 1960s, this Society absorbed the Primitive Methodists from the Jubilee Chapel. The other chapel belonging to the United Methodist Church is in Framwellgate Moor. The foundation stone for its first chapel was laid in 1869 and a Sunday School was added in 1902. The closure of the colliery in 1924 resulted in considerable loss of members, but an increase in the local population later, combined with the closure of the Primitive Methodist Chapel and the Wesleyan Methodist Chapel in Pity Me, gave the Society a new lease of life. It built a new chapel in 1959. There was a small society with a stone chapel in New Durham, which was established in 1838, when the chapel was built. It closed in 1911 and the chapel was demolished.

The Durham City Corps (No 156) of the Salvation Army was one of the earliest established in the country. It was first housed in a cellar under the shops on Elvet Bridge, being known as the 'Old Glory Shop'. Before meetings the officer had to go down, deal with the vermin and then sweep out. Later the Corps had a building in Claypath, since removed by the new Sunderland Road. It then crossed the river and occupied the old Wesleyan Methodist Chapel in Old Elvet until it moved to its present premises in Saddler Street in 1925.

The Roman Catholic community has always been present in Durham since the Reformation. Initially it was probably fairly large and reflected those who did not wish to change to the 'new way'. They were served by itinerant priests, who covered the whole county, masses presumably being said in private houses. Despite a brief relaxation in Queen Mary's reign (1553-8) the priests were hunted down and, when caught, were hanged, drawn and quartered like traitors. One of these courageous men was John Boste, canonised in 1970, who served the Catholic community of England and, in particular, northern England, well. He was caught immediately after celebrating mass at the Waterhouse, near Esh in October 1593. In the course of the following ten months he was subjected to a series of tortures and interrogations in York and London. Eventually he was returned to Durham to stand trial on 23 July 1594. After a confession of guilt, he was taken to Dryburn, where he was hanged for about twenty seconds, taken down and carried to the fire. 'The actual movement caused Boste to revive, although he had undergone partial strangulation by the rope, and with a slurred voice forgave the executioners. Boste was was then disembowelled, quartered and his quarters boiled'. The intensity of priest hunting seems to have relaxed somewhat following the accession of James I. Instead, the members of the Church were required to pay their fines for non-attendance at the parish church. This system produced considerable revenue, but was open to abuse. In 1627 Catholics were able to compound for their annual fines, and it is from the lists of recusants and those compounding that it is possible to demonstrate that Durham City formed one of three centres of Catholicism in the county.

By 1685 Durham was not only a centre of Catholicism, but also had at least one chapel. The Maire family bought a house in Gilesgate probably in 1662-3, and held services there until the late eighteenth century when, by a complex legal device, the property was left to the secular clergy. In Old Elvet there were two chapels and a chaplaincy. The chapels were at 33 Old Elvet (John Forcer's house) which had a public chapel from at least 1685, (in 1725 this property came into the hands of the secular clergy), and Nos 44-5 Old Elvet, in the hands of the Jesuits from before 1688 until they disposed of it in the 1820s. It seems that there was a chapel here in 1688 when it was destroyed by a mob. The chaplaincy was that of Mary, Lady Ratcliffe, daughter of the Earl of Derwentwater, who built a house now incorporated in the County Hotel, in 1698. She seems to have had a chaplain resident from about 1705 until about 1730. Part of his duties included teaching a school, apparently for young ladies.

Until 1826 there were two Catholic chapels in the City, both in Old Elvet. On 31 May 1827 a new church was opened, dedicated to St Cuthbert. At that point it did not have a spire, which was added in 1869, together with a Lady Chapel. By the mid-nineteenth century there was considerable pressure on space, because of the increase in Catholic immigrants, principally Irish. In 1857 land, including the Wheatsheaf Inn, was bought in Framwellgate for a mission. A temporary church capable of holding up to five hundred people was erected, employing the dining room of the house and a wooden shed erected to one side of it. Eventually enough money was raised for a new church, which was opened in 1864 and dedicated to St Godric. Five years later St Godric's was established as a separate parish. Members of the large Catholic community were buried in the churchyards of their respective Anglican churches until 1866, when a Catholic burial ground was opened on the Red Hills. The following year the cemetery chapel dedicated to St Bede was opened.

The nonconformist churches responded quickly to the dramatic changes in the population around Durham. The Church of England, less flexible than the nonconformists, responded to the situation by building a new church on the New North Road. Dedicated to St Cuthbert, it was opened in 1863. St Mary Magdalene, built for a similar reason in Belmont, was opened in 1857.

Rationalisation and amalgamation have led to a steadily decreasing number of chapels in Durham. On the outskirts, however, there have been two new additions. A third Catholic church, dedicated to St Joseph, has been built in Gilesgate Moor and, at Newton Hall, the newest of all the suburbs, the Anglican and Methodist communities share a single church.

There was a small Jewish community in Durham from 1888. In the late 1890s a small place of worship was established in John Street, when there were 72 members drawn from about fifteen families. Numbers increased and, by 1909, the congregation was too large for the John Street premises. A permanent synagogue was built and opened in Laburnum Avenue in 1910, when there were 107 in the Durham community. The community soon started to fall in numbers and after 1918 it struggled to survive. Eventually the synagogue was closed and sold in 1955.

LEFT: Christopher Hodgson's mould for a bell still in St Oswald's tower. Found during excavations in the Blacksmiths Shop, Durham Cathedral by Julian Bennett. (TM) BELOW: St Margaret's church, 1824; Joseph Bouet. RIGHT: St Mary-the-Less in 1824, Joseph Bouet. (Both DC Add MS 95)

ABOVE: St Mary-le-Bow in 1824, Joseph Bouet. (DC Add MS 95). BELOW: In 1669 there was a national 'census' of Dissenting Meeting Houses. The individual returns by parish still survive, together with the Archdeacon of Durham's report to Bishop Cosin, and Bishop Cosin's report, in Lambeth Palace. This return is for a group of Quakers meeting in John Heighington's house, probably in Claypath, on 11 July 1669. The Friends Meeting House in Claypath was built in 1679. (DPAD: PK; Post-Dissolution Loose Papers, Box 30)

ABOVE: Presbyterian Chapel, Claypath, built in 1750. (KEP) RIGHT: Claypath Congregational Church (now United Reformed) built in 1893. (PAGC) CENTRE: Salvation Army Citadel, Saddler Street. BELOW LEFT: Neville's Cross (Primitive) Methodist chapel, closed 1980. (Both KEP) RIGHT: St Godric's Roman Catholic church after a fire in 1984. (PAGC)

Behind The Mask

Not everything is as it seems. Centuries of Durham builders' work are there to be seen, but while in most cases Durham's buildings are not disguised, in a surprisingly high proportion the real building is concealed by a later mask. Good examples of this are City Sports in the Market Place where a timber-framed building is hidden by a Victorian frontage, or the humbler, almost cottage-like exterior of 79 Saddler Street, now the southern portion of Crawford's Restaurant, which seems to belong to the early nineteenth century. Nothing could be further from the truth, for the frontage conceals two separate seventeenth century timber-framed houses set one behind the other. The front one is built along the street, while the back one is set at right angles to the street.

They were both built in the early seventeenth century with separate accesses from the street, the front building having access direct from the street, while the rear one had access from a vennel or alleyway which ran up the southern side of the front building to a yard behind. A second vennel ran off this alley between the two buildings and onto only these two houses. Even now the jetties on the upper floors over this alley are visible. The rear house suffered somewhat, later in the seventeenth century, but the front house preserves one of a pair of dormer windows over the alley. There was another pair facing out to Saddler Street, which has since been removed. In the later seventeenth century, the two houses were united by a steep stair filling the vennel between. On the first floor there is a small landing with a door to each house, while a grander landing on the second floor leads into two rooms in each. The third floor rooms of both are connected by a gallery. Each of the top floor rooms has a stone and brick fireplace inserted probably somewhere between the seventeenth and nineteenth centuries. The stairs at the third floor cut through one of the dormer windows of the front house, while the other one was transformed to serve as the doorway into the northern of the two rooms. It leads straight onto the gallery and then into the single third floor room of the rear house, which has a seventeenth century door secured by a pair of strap hinges. The walls of the two buildings that face the stair seem to have been torn down, apart from the main structural timbers, when the stair was put in and then rebuilt with close studding, just visible in places. All the door frames probably belong to this late seventeenth century work, though only the two third floor doors facing onto the gallery are probably of that date. The back wall of the rear house is of stone and had a fireplace in it on the ground floor.

The second floor of the front house has a marvellous early seventeenth century plaster ceiling in what was the northern of a pair of rooms. The front of the building was supported on a pair of massive timbers that were removed with great difficulty to make way for a modern shop front in 1977. Another major alteration to the building was the change of access to the upper floors. Before 1977 the sole access was by the side entry and up the late seventeenth century stairs. Now there is direct access from the street front.

This is but one of a number of timber-framed buildings that line Saddler Street. Most of the buildings from Coyne's (now Crawfords) down to No 79 show signs of concealed timber-framing. Indeed, when Coynes was converted during 1983 it was possible to see the remains of the timber-framed house which had been almost completely replaced by a later brick-built house and shop. This property was one of a pair of buildings, one behind the other, the rear one of nineteenth century date. The gap between the two was filled by a stair. The House of Andrews (now Martins) next door, and separated by an alleyway, is again at least two properties separated by a stair filling the vennel between front and rear houses (this is the stair leading up to the House of Andrews Restaurant). These buildings seem to have been stone on the ground floor, though the rear building is timber framed above. Further buildings surround the small courtyard behind the restaurant and perhaps this is where Aynesly made his mustard in the nineteenth century.

The obviously timber-framed house at No 32 Silver Street has some surprises, for the building is four storeys high above the street but six storeys high above Back Silver Street. The lower three storeys are all stone-built, the next two are timber-framed, while the top storey is a later brick addition of the nineteenth century. The timber-framed section was probably built in the earlier seventeenth century on top of the earlier stone section. The stone-built basement of 26 Silver Street was probably late medieval or early post-medieval in date. It may be that most of the cellars along this side of the street represent earlier houses with later superstructures. Perhaps the most intriguing building is 30 Silver Street, built over a void, which was in living memory a vennel leading down from Silver Street to Back Silver Street.

When Woolworths was extended in 1960 one of the buildings demolished proved to have been a stone-built seventeenth century house. There are rather more surviving stone houses built in the seventeenth century than we realise, frequently hidden by a nineteenth or even twentieth century facade, or else lying out of sight, such as the ruined building on Moatside Lane which was converted into four one-roomed dwellings, each with its own oven, in the nineteenth century.

Beyond the City centre fewer early buildings survive. In Claypath many properties have the print of the late eighteenth or nineteenth century builders' hand, but there may be scraps of earlier ones hidden away. A prime example is the fragment of timber-framing embedded in the boundary wall between Blue Coat and Bailes Yards. The western suburbs have suffered most from the hands of the developer. In the nineteenth century the New North Road was driven through the suburb. This century much of Framwellgate was demolished as part of a slum clearance programme in the 1930s. From recent excavation it would seem that the buildings then cleared (referred to as 'rookeries' in reports of Council meetings in 1930) were probably first built in the seventeenth century. There were certainly two sixteenth century cottages that went in that clearance. More recently still, the Millburngate Development removed a number of buildings of which the Jewellery Centre, with its rebuilt timber framing and stone structure, was the sole survivor.

Spacious, gracious Old Elvet is the epitome of eighteenth century Durham to outward appearances, though we may expect to discover earlier buildings hidden within the later ones. The County Hotel has absorbed the 1808 Wesleyan Chapel and also a pair of seventeenth century stairs, one imported. The only part of the two Elvets to openly preserve their early character is at the bridgehead where the bridge still supports houses. Further uphill New Elvet is indeed new, containing the University's large complex of lecture rooms and Dunelm House, replacing the earlier houses that once stood there. Above that, however, Hallgarth Street presents a humble eighteenth or early nineteenth century face to the world and conceals its treasures. No 56, for example, preserved the original clay floor beneath the later wooden floor until recently, and embedded in the structure were three separate stairs of which only one was functional. This building also conceals a sixteenth or early seventeenth century chimney. The best hidden treasure of them all is, of course, the Priors Manor House, which became known as Hallgarth Farm and is now partly the Prison Officer's Club. The medieval tithe barn with a stone ground floor and timber-framed upper floor forms part of that club.

There are three buildings lying slightly beyond the bounds of the City and its suburbs which are important because of their direct connection with the City and its institutions. The fourteenth century gateway to Kepier Hospital, with the late sixteenth century loggia still surviving from Heath's remodelling of the hospital, is all that stands to remind us of a grander past. With no need of a memorial is the magnificent group of buildings at Crook Hall, which contain the remains of a series of manor houses built between the thirteenth and eighteenth centuries. The farm buildings in the western part of the complex consist of a sixteenth or seventeenth century byre or barn, a cart shed and a remarkable late eighteenth century granary, which has recently been sensitively converted to a house. On the east side of the wide track which served the farmstead are further farmbuildings and the hall itself. Situated on the north side of the seventeenth century walled gardens, the hall is a linear progression of structures dating from the thirteenth to the late eighteenth century. The west wing is the eighteenth century hall, first built in 1730, of which only the kitchen and stair remain, and then rebuilt to form the elegant building that is there today. It was connected to the earlier medieval hall by the remains of a seventeenth century building rebuilt after a fire in 1671. All that remains of the seventeenth century structures are the entrance at the medieval end with an attendant passageway, a room containing not only an enormous fireplace but a distinctive sixteenth century stair of diagonally cut timbers and, most surprisingly, the remains of a floral pattern in red on a white ground, painted on the joists of the first floor. In the narrow passage connecting this room to the eighteenth century hall is a large window which, when unblocked in 1976, proved to be still glazed with its seventeenth century diamond lattice of lead cames and some of the diamond-shaped quarries. It is possible that this belonged to a building extending under the later hall, which was demolished in the eighteenth century.

It is more than likely that the seventeenth century hall used parts of the medieval structure, including a wing projecting to the north from the single room that survives from this hall. Certainly, it reused (in the entrance passage) the external wall of the west end of the original, as well as a free standing timber-framed wall on a low clay-bonded stone base, which may be all that is left of an even earlier building. The hall, lit by five lancet lights with triple cusps in the heads, had at one time a newel stair on the exterior face of the east wall. A blocked doorway in the south east corner leads out into what was once another part of the hall, but is now only a heap of rubble (overgrown) and the bottom courses of the south wall. These now serve as the bottom courses of the north wall in the eastern half of walled garden. It is clear, too, that the medieval complex extended further north than today, for there is a door in the north wall of the hall and the remains of walls reflecting an earlier, possibly medieval, north-south building were recently seen beneath the seventeenth century hall. The interest of this manor house lies not just in its remarkable survival but also in the fact that the piped water supply for Durham City came from the Fram Well on the land of Sidegate Manor in 1450, and continued to function well into the nineteenth century.

The third building peripheral to Durham is the Prior's manor house at Beaurepaire, some 1½ miles west of the City centre. This served as the principal country house of the Priors of Durham from the later thirteenth century until the Dissolution. The manor house was first built for Prior Bertram of Middleton, when he retired through corporeal infirmity in 1358. It then consisted of the Prior's lodging, a chapel and a kitchen and larder. In the mid-fourteenth century the manor house was considerably enlarged, when it possibly achieved its final form of three western wings attached to an eastern courtyard with ranges of rooms round it. The manor house survived to roof height until the late eighteenth century, and then in the space of about forty years collapsed, leaving only a little more than could be seen in 1980. Since then a campaign of excavation jointly funded by the University, City and County Councils has resulted in the discovery of substantial remains. The manor house in its inner court occupied about six acres, while the entire complex of inner and outer courts covers about thirty-eight acres. The outer court had a gateway near Stotgate Farm and held a series of buildings, principally agricultural, demolished by the Scots army in 1640 and 1644. It was regularly used by the monks of Durham during the *ludi*, which were periods of relaxation from full rule, *ie* holidays.

The focal point of the City has always been the Market Place. In the late twelfth century the Bishop's tenants were required to build booths in Durham at the major fairs of the year on St Cuthbert's day. These took place in Market Place or The Sands. The regular weekly markets were regulated by the Bishop's officers until the Incorporation of the Borough, and then by members of the Corporation through the Court of Pye Powder on fair days. Otherwise the regulation will have been overseen by at least the Bishop's officers until the 1602 charter. The administration and regulation of the individual crafts had to a large extent passed into the hands of the craft guilds themselves by the fifteenth century, so the Bishop's officers were left with affairs concerning weights and measures and collection of tolls.

In 1555 Bishop Tunstall erected a Town Hall on the west side of the Market Place, replacing the earlier Tollbooth. His building was largely replaced by Bishop Cosin in 1665, altered in 1752 and again in 1754. Eventually in 1849 it was decided that a completely new Town Hall was needed. Consequently the 'old erection which was dingy and decaying was restored, care being taken to preserve as much of the interior as was consistent with the improvement'. A new Town Hall was added, built to the designs of P. C. Hardwick of London. It was completed and formally opened on 29 January 1851 at a civic banquet.

In the Market Place itself was a large stone cross which was erected at the expense of Thomas Emmerson of London in 1617. It had a large pillar in the middle, ornamented with a sun dial. It became ruinous and in 1780 the Corporation ordered its removal. The materials were used to build a Piazza as the market for corn and provisions. This survived until 1854 when it was dismantled, since its function had largely been replaced by the new markets erected on the west side of the Market Place 'somewhat after the mannor of a railway station, being lighted and ventilated from the roof and sides'.

An important part of the Market Place was the source of water for public use. This was the pant supplied by piped water from the Fram Well in Sidegate Manor, constructed initially in 1450 when the agreement between the townspeople and Thomas Billlingham allowed the water to come to the Market Place in pipes. Only Billingham's descendants could take pipes thence to their houses. It was replaced at an unspecified date by a stone octagonal pant which had a statue of Neptune added in 1729. In the mid-nineteenth century control of the pant passed from the pantmasters elected by the vestry of St Nicholas Church to the Local Board of Health's Pant Committee. In 1853 a letter to the Committee complained that, since the head of the Fram Well had been sunk deeper and the lead pipes replaced with iron ones (in 1847) the water in the Market Place had become unfit for human consumption. It took the Pant Committee until 1860 to act, when a competition was held to design a new fountain. In Janaury 1861 the Committee considered designs. It finally opted for E. R. Robon's designs in 1863 (as the Fountain Committee) and also considered (and rejected) the possibility of forgoing a free-standing fountain for two plain ones on either side of the statue of the Marquess of Londonderry erected in 1861. It was replaced again in 1900 and finally demolished in 1923, when the statue of Neptune was removed to Wharton Park.

Motorised traffic made the Market Place an increasingly dangerous area, as the magistrates noted in 1930 when fining 'bus drivers for picking up passengers other than at authorised stages. Access to the Market Place up Silver Street was so bad in that year that serious proposals were made to demolish either all the houses on the north side of the street or, at the least, to demolish a few key properties. Ultimately, the decision was made to install traffic lights. Later, a traffic control point was erected in the Market Place around which traffic turned to go up Saddler Street. The traffic lights on Elvet Bridge and Silver Street were operated by a policeman in the Market Place, latterly assisted by television cameras. Once the new Elvet Bridge had been opened, the way was open to remove traffic altogether. Since 1974 the town centre has become increasingly pedestrian-dominated, a return to earlier days, though without the risk of being ridden down by horses as happened to Agnes, wife of John of the Castle, cook, in 1344 when she miscarried.

Axonometric drawing showing the timbers and the infilled vennel between the two houses at INSET: 79 Saddler Street.

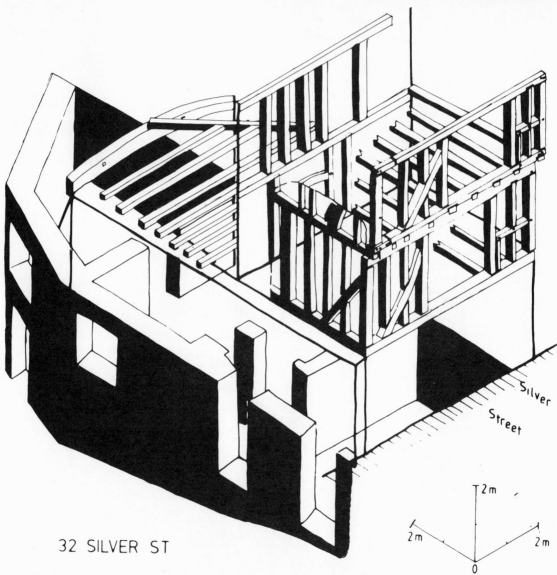

32 SILVER ST

2m

2m

2m

0

OPPOSITE ABOVE LEFT: Roof timbers and RIGHT: early 17th century ceiling in 79 Saddler Street. (PAGC) BELOW: Axonometric drawing of 32 Silver Street. LEFT ABOVE: 17th century floor boards still in situ in 32 Silver Street (and even now trapped between the ground floor ceiling and the first floor floor!) BELOW: 32 Silver Street in 1886. RIGHT: Fragment of a timber-framed building in Blue Coat School Yard off Claypath. (PAGC). BELOW: Timber-framed building in Owengate. (DUAD)

LEFT: Hallgarth Tithe Barn, watercolour by E. W. Claughan, 1891, (original in the possession of Mr J. Myres). RIGHT: Kepier Hospital 14th century gateway. (DCC) BELOW: The loggia of Kepier Inn built in the 16th century by John Heath. (DCC)

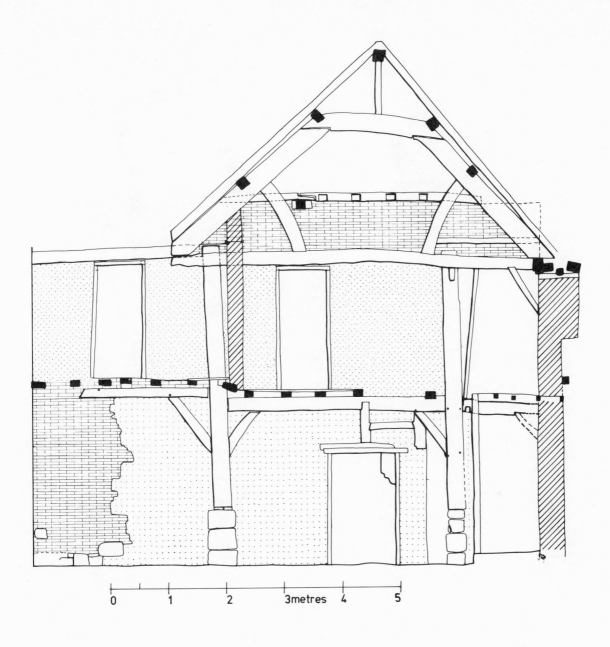

Elevation of early timber-framed wall between the medieval and 17th
century portions of the Hall.

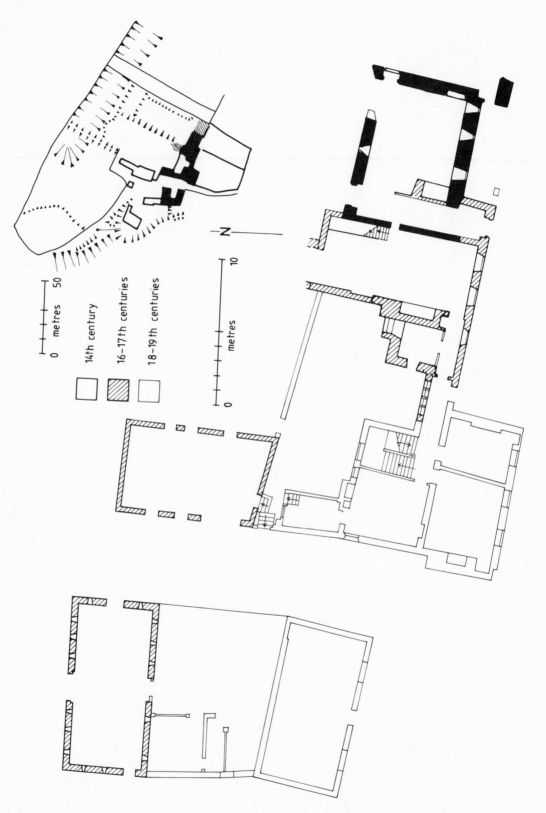

14th century

16-17th centuries

18-19th centuries

0   metres   50

0   metres   10

N

Plan of Crook Hall.

108

Crook Hall: ABOVE LEFT: windows in the medieval hall in 1976; RIGHT: medieval timber-framing with an infill of clay-bonded stonework; BELOW LEFT: three stairs in the 17th century portion, laid one on top of the other. The latest is 19th century while the earliest is 16th or 17th century, the treads being made of logs quartered lengthwise. RIGHT: 17th century painting survives on a number of beams. (All PAGC)

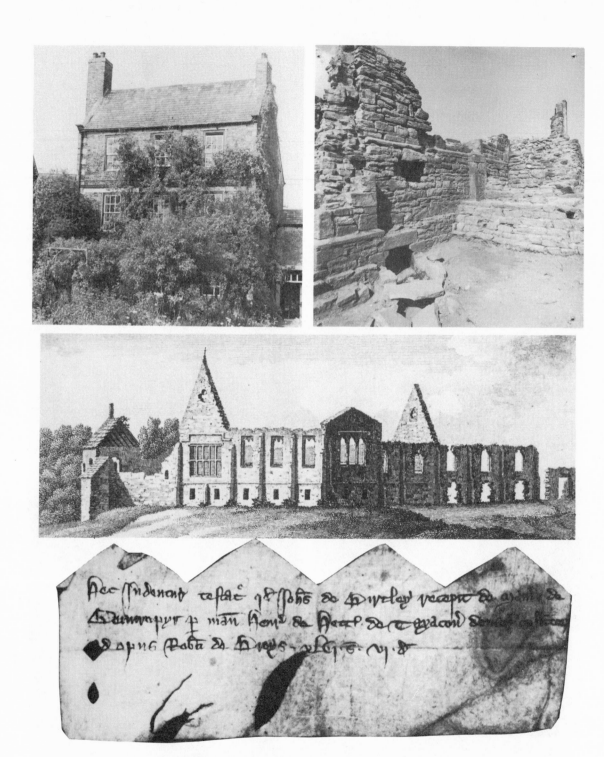

LEFT: Crook Hall: the Georgian Hall; RIGHT: the south-west corner of the Prior's lodging at his manor house of Beaurepaire after excavation in 1982. (PAGC) CENTRE: The ruins of Beaurepaire as they stood in 1787: this is the area excavated. BELOW: In 1326 the Scots army invaded County Durham but was bought off when it reached Beaurepaire. This receipt shows that 46s 6d was collected from Beaurepaire as a contribution to the blackmail. (DPAD: PK; Misc Ch 4605)

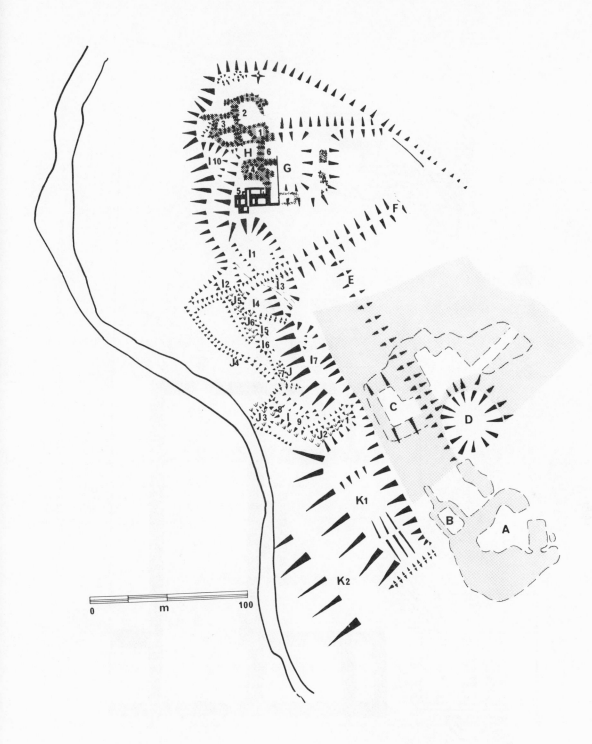

Plan showing just over half of the manor house complex at Beaurepaire.

Legend:

- **1258** (solid black)
- late 13th C.
- early 14th C.
- mid 14th C.
- 16th C.

0   5   metres   10

Plan of the exposed buildings (excavated 1980-1984) at Beaurepaire.

With Due Care

There were two hospitals (Kepier and St Mary Magdalene) in the medieval period, not to serve the sick, but to relieve the poor. Kepier in its 1180 refounding had an establishment of thirteen brethren of whom six were chaplains, and the remaining seven were concerned with the administration of the lands, goods and services of the hospital: these included a tanyard, mills (both that on the Millburn and that granted later in the twelfth century on the Wear) and a baking oven. It is likely that there were thirteen inmates — latterly perhaps more pensioners of the King and Bishop than those in dire need — but these were supplemented by paying guests, pilgrims to St Cuthbert. By 1306 the poor and strangers were constantly resorting to the hospital. Ten years later, as a consequence of the foundation of the prebend of Kepier in Auckland College, its revenues went to feed an extra ten paupers at the hospital every evening. One of the last endowments was in 1445, when Bishop Neville appropriated the rectory of St Nicholas together with its glebe at Old Durham to the hospital in exchange for tithe corn payments.

The buildings included an infirmary, common dormitory and common hall in the later twelfth century. The whole structure was rebuilt in the mid-fourteenth century. This was a period of crisis, for in 1355 Bishop Hatfield granted an Indulgence to all who contributed to the relief of the hospital 'in consequence of the plague among the tenants of the hospital, failure of the crops and murrain among the cattle'.

The hospital was dissolved in 1546 and its possessions passed to the Crown, to be sold to the laity. It came into the hands of John Heath, Warden of the Fleet, in 1568. He died in 1591 and his splendid effigy is to be seen in the chancel of St Giles Church. His son John built a house, latterly known as Kepier Inn, which stood on the site of the hospital until relatively recently. All that now remains is the imposing gateway and the elegant loggia of Heath's house in the orchard.

The hospital of St Mary Magdalene was founded as the result of a donation of land by John de Hameldon to the Prior and Convent of Durham, for procuring masses for himself and his family. After some initial difficulties over exchanges of land between the Priory and Kepier Hospital, a settlement was arrived at, probably in the 1230s or 1240s, whereby twelve acres of Kepier land called Southcroft, on the north side of Gilesgate, were ceded to the Priory as well as lands elsewhere, and the revenues used for the benefit of the souls of John de Hameldon and all departed. It is clear that the twelve acres of Southcroft were used to build to chapel and hospital. In the early fourteenth century, the hospital was founded for a chaplain, and thirteen brethren and sisters who were needy persons of good character, who had seen better days.

In 1370 the Almoner of the Priory spent considerable sums on repairing walls, re-roofing, painting the image of St Mary Magdalene, making a chamber for a chaplain, glazing a window and in making a barn. This work was not to last, for the chapel was built on wet ground and by 1448 was ruinous from the weakness of the foundations. On 2 February 1449 Bishop Neville licensed Prior and Convent to pull it down and rebuild elsewhere in the hospital's territory. The new chapel was erected a little to the west of the old one. The cost of the work was high and included painting the image of the Blessed Mary Magdalene (16s 1d) and a payment of £2 0 0d to John Chambre of York for glass and painting. Timber came from the Priory's estate at Beaurepaire and elsewhere. The church was also provided with a bell and walled churchyard.

By the sixteenth century there seem only to have been a chaplain and four residents in the hospital, whose chapel was still being re-roofed as late as 1554. The church had been served by the Master of the Prior's School for poor boys outside the Abbey Gates; he was required to say mass twice a week. After the Dissolution the services were maintained by the Dean and Chapter until 'some time after the Restoration [1660] the Church, having been allowed to fall into ruin, its services were discontinued and the stipend of £4 annexed to the office of Librarian'.

After the Dissolution of the Monasteries the Parish was the focus for the relief of the poor and sick. The core of its funds came from the poor rate, but this was enhanced by numerous charitable bequests. Probably the largest such bequest was that of Henry Smith, who left his coal mines (worth £100 a year) and other property worth £600 to the Corporation. This substantial endowment arose because Smith's daughter had been converted to Roman Catholicism, having witnessed the execution of four priests in 1590, and had then married into one of the leading Catholic families of the County. Smith, who died in 1598, stipulated that the revenues were to be used 'chieflie that some good trade may be devised for the setting of youth and other idle persons to work as shal be thought most convenient, wherby some profitts may arise to the benefitt of this Cittie, and reliefe of those that are at worke, and have lived honestlie upon their trade'.

In 1612 New Place, the Neville's 'palace' was bought and used for a cloth manufactory until 1619 or 1620, when it was closed, and in its stead £20 a year was paid to the poor, and ten or more apprentices were bound out each year. Between 1616 and 1620 the master of the House of Correction received sums to purchase wool, so that children might spin it. The capital of the endowment was used to purchase land and property and the rents used for the charitable purposes specified by Smith. In 1760 it was decreed that the revenue should be used, among other things, to encourage and promote 'the worsted manufactory then carried on in the City'. In fact the governors of the charity bought the building used for the factory and this later became Henderson's dye house.

Another charitable foundation standing in the mainstream of the medieval custom is the almshouse founded by Bishop Cosin in 1666 and still in existence. It was established for four men and four women, all to be appointed by the Bishop out of the poor of Durham, with the exception of two who were to come from the Parish of Brancepeth. Bishop Cosin built the almshouse on Palace Green. It was moved in 1877 to its present location off Owengate, when the University took over the older premises.

The first hospital in Durham in the modern sense was St Leonard's, founded before 1292 as a leper hospital at the top of what is now North Road. In 1404 there was only one leper in residence. Criminals hanged at Dryburn were buried in its grounds even after its demolition in 1652-3. The burials took place in and around the site of the Garden House public house — work there in recent years has disturbed human remains. Otherwise there seems not to have been a hospital for the relief of the sick until the Dispensary was founded in Saddler Street in 1785. Popular demand and financial support were such that the Trustees decided to build an Infirmary. This was built on land granted by William Wilkinson in 1793 in Crossgate. It had a resident house-surgeon, matron and apothecary to care for the eighty in-patients and four hundred or more out-patients treated each year. A subscription of one guinea entitled the subscriber to recommend two out-patients a year; two guineas ensured one in-patient or four out-patients. The Infirmary closed after the County Hospital was opened in 1853, again on Mr Wilkinson's land. At that time there were forty-four in-patients and a steadily increasing number of out-patients who gained access to the hospital through the recommendation of a subscriber. In 1867 male and female convalescent wings were added and named after Dean Waddington as a memorial to his munificence in establishing and maintaining the hospital. Other wards were added through the liberality of John Eden and the hospital was again extended in 1938.

At the head of Crossgate is a geriatric hospital, St Margaret's, which started life as the workhouse in 1837. In 1870 an Infirmary and fever hospital were erected adjoining the original building. Twenty-one years later, part of the first building was demolished to make way for a new dining hall. There were two other hospitals, which have now gone. The first was the No 5 Durham Voluntary Association Hospital located at 17 North Bailey between 1914 and early 1919. The other was the Durham Public Assistance Institution, at the junction of Castle Chare and North Road until its demolition in 1967. This three-storeyed building had ten small wards for eighty-three patients, principally the chronic sick. Dryburn Hospital started life as a temporary hospital in 1938 but rapidly grew and is still with us.

In 1819 the gaol moved from the Castle's North Gate to its present location at the east end of Old Elvet. The new prison incorporated the House of Correction, which had been at the west end of Elvet Bridge on the site of St James' chapel since at least 1632. Towards the end of the eighteenth century it was abundantly clear that very considerable improvements were needed in the gaol's accommodation, for it was over-crowded, ill-ventilated and a breeding-ground for disease and criminals. Convicted male prisoners — as well as those awaiting trial — were held together, sharing a sleeping apartment (in reality a dungeon) and a day room on the top floor of the gaol. The women only had one room by 1818, whereas before 1802 they, too, had had a dungeon to sleep in. Those debtors able to pay for accommodation were allotted individual or (at a cheaper rate) shared rooms and had a small courtyard. Debtors without means were confined to two rooms 10'4" square.

In 1809 the foundation stones of a new Assize Court and Prison were laid. The Assize Court opened in 1811 and the prison in 1819. The buildings were erected to the designs of Ignatius Bonomi after two other architects had been dismissed. The prison was so arranged that the debtors were housed in the west wing, female felons in the east wing and male felons in a spacious building on the south side. Water was supplied from a seventy feet deep well in the courtyard. In 1834 the felons were employed in beating flax, weaving blankets and cloth and breaking stone by hand. The treadmill was only used occasionally. In 1870 the prisoners were in cells which doubled as workshops, where they were employed in making mats or teasing oakum 'which is greatly disliked'.

The Rules for the Government of Durham Gaol in 1824 give a clear indication of the concern for cleanliness and order. Three times a year the prisoners had to scrape and limewash the walls and ceilings of the wards, cells, rooms and passages. Each room and ward was swept daily and washed once a week from Michaelmas to Lady Day and twice a week or oftener if needed from Lady Day to Michaelmas. Every morning the windows and doors of sleeping cells were opened and bed clothes hung up and aired. Before attending chapel each morning, every prisoner had to washing his or her hands and face and comb his or her hair; they could not have breakfast until this had been done. A sufficient supply of soap, towels and combs was provided. While there was clean body linen every week, blankets and rugs were washed in the week after every Quarter Sessions, presumably a necessity since the Rules make no mention of sheets.

The prison had originally been designed for seventy to eighty prisoners but, as the century progressed, so the number of inmates increased and perhaps the 1824 regulation of no more than three men to a cell was transgressed. The time came when the prison had to be internally re-organised. In 1870, William Crozier, the County Architect, saw to it that no aspect was ignored, even to the extent of introducing air conditioning. George Walker described the system: 'The cells containing about nine hundred and twenty cubic feet, they are warmed when the weather requires it, and the least quantity of air admitted is twenty-one cubic feet per minute, the amount being ascertained by an anemometer'.

While no little care was taken to ensure that justice was done according to the law of the day through the courts (on the west side of Palace Green until 1808), the released prisoners were shunned by Society, particularly in the Victorian era. The difficulties of finding gainful employment, especially for women, were so formidable that the freed prisoner was likely only to find a welcome among the criminal fraternity. The prison chaplain in 1840, George Hans Harrison, was aware of this and helped prisoners of good intent and whose needs were genuine. He either found them work or supported them until they found it. Girls were accommodated in the Assistant School Master's house, where they learnt knitting and other useful skills until they could be placed in service. Harrison was helped by others, and together they formed an informal society. One of its immediately visible products was the Penitentiary in Gilesgate in 1853. This was founded and maintained by public subscription with no little support from Dean Waddington and Roland Burdon MP. A guide to the City in 1920 described the Penitentiary as having done 'a great deal of useful work in reclaiming those upon whom Society as a whole looks on with scorn'.

The less visible work of the group gathered around Harrison was the creation of a refuge for released prisoners, helping them find work, clothes and tools. He left Durham Prison in 1854 and this side of his work was not continued for long. However, in 1882 the Discharged Prisoners Aid Society was formed with the encouragement of the Board of Prison Commissioners. The Society's agent, who had established a network of contacts in the county to find employment for ex-prisoners, became effective in persuading men to sign the Pledge. The importance of this is seen, when one considers that in 1902, 91% of all prison sentences in Durham were due to drunkenness. A particular concern of the Society since the first decade of this century has been young offenders, especially those in Borstal. In 1925 the Prison Governor said of the young prisoner 'he does not know what work is and sees no connection between it and daily bread. Two or three years ago he left school and has loafed about the streets since'.

The Society's work continued unabated, especially once it had bought 19 Old Elvet as a refuge for women and a place for breakfast on the day of release. It now exists as a purely voluntary organisation with no official grants or duties and provides, through 19 Old Elvet, a hostel for ex-prisoners and for visiting families.

The DPAS did not work in isolation, for it had close contact with a number of other benevolent societies which shared some of its aims. Some were of long standing and others had a relatively short life. Nevertheless, when in being, they were an important, not to say essential, part of pre-Welfare State Society. Two such were the Mendicity Society which had a soup kitchen in Moatside Lane, and the Durham Diocesan Association for the Care of Friendless Women and Girls. This established St Catherine's House in Framwellgate as a refuge for women and girls in moral danger. Individuals too, had their part to play in relieving distress, especially earlier this century. For many years, Harry Murdoch, Alderman and Mayor (1929-30) held an annual Christmas dinner for four hundred old people in the Town Hall. Mayor W. W. Wilkinson in 1928-9 organised a collection, separate from the

Mayor's Charity, which allowed for the distribution of 60,000 articles of clothing, blankets and boots to the distressed poor in 1928 alone.

The Victorians had noted an inseparable connection between filth, misery, vice and crime. Recognising also the connection between filfth and the killers cholera, typhus and smallpox, they set about removing the causes. The first stage in Durham was a report on the sanitary condition of the City to the General Board of Health in 1849. This found that Moatside Lane, for example, was unpaved and had open gutters into which the house slops were thrown. The upper houses also drained onto the lower. The Market Place had drains which discharged onto Back Silver Street and Back Lane 'where they fill an open, offensive gutter, which beyond St Nicholas' church ends in an open and exposed stagnant ditch. Further on is a large depot for the street sweepings of a part of the town, which include soil and filth thrown out from houses onto the street'. Paradise Lane was set about with 'open gutters and ditches, ash-pits and other nuisances . . . and in Paradise Garden below is a considerable manure deposit'. The dung hill was there by 1802.

On the west side of the town the filth from the east side of South Street, Framwellgate and Milburngate was thrown down the river bank while houses on the west side of those streets simply discharged into the street. Allergate had an open gutter and a large offensive gutter grate, the drain from which discharged and flooded a footpath between Allergate and North Road. The Millburn crossed North Road at its bottom end where it collected a large quantity of material from drains. This was brought to the surface between two houses newly built shortly before 1849 and then collected in the old mill pool.

In Elvet the courts and places occupied by the poorer classes were characterised by open privies and piggeries. Water Lane had not only an open cess pool in the middle of the road, but a common lodging house which had thirteen or fourteen people to the room. The eastern end of Elvet Bridge was noted as a considerable nuisance, since the drains from the houses on the bridge discharged directly onto the piers below. The nuisance was only abated when the river was running high.

The principal function of the Local Board of Health in its early years was to eradicate these dangers to the public health. One of them was the Race Course 'That used to be one of the pleasantest walks in Durham formerly, when there were neither police nor inspectors'. This anonymous correspondent to the Board brought its attention to the fact that drains from the south side of Elvet at that end were simply discharging onto the back lane there and filtering onto the Race Course.

The keeping of pigs either in piggeries or singly was a nuisance that sixteen people were ordered to abate in the last three months of 1853: two each in Claypath, Gilesgate and Providence Row, five in Crossgate, four in Framwellgate and one piggery on Elvet Bridge. In that same period 73 other nuisance notices were served, of which thirty were for Framwellgate and a further twenty for Claypath and New Elvet.

As the Board of Health replaced open gutters with proper sewers, so the householders along the street were required to put in a drain connecting the house to the sewer at a specified depth and fall. In October and November of 1853, for example, the occupiers of houses on Crossgate, Allergate, North Road and Framwellgate were required to install their drains.

In September of that year, William Robson, the Superintendent of Police, had inspected houses occupied by the Irish. Of 798 Irish in the town, 324 lived in Framwellgate and 207 in the City proper. He noted that several of the dwellings were clean and orderly 'whilst others are extremely dirty, more so than the worst of the common lodging houses.

'The want of Air, ventilation and cleanliness is keenly perceptible on approaching many of these habitations, and several of there Children whose nakedness is scarcely covered with rags are allowed to waller in filth. The effluvia in the interior of the dwellings is most noxious, and can scarcely fail to engender sickliness and desease. Personal cleanliness being appearintly altogathir unknown to them'.

The Board of Health performed a wide range of services for Durham. Not only was it concerned with public health, but it dealt with scavenging, street cleaning, lighting and paving, public water supply and sewage as well as the fire service. In 1857 the Sewerage, Paving, Flagging and Road Committee of the Board resolved that a gas lamp be placed 'on the corner of Mrs McNally's Schoolroom on the South side of the Methodist Chapel passage' (in Elvet). This is merely one of many instances in which the committee determined where each gas lamp in the City was to be placed or moved. Indeed, in 1930 the City Council was still making just the same type of decision. It recommended that a lamp be placed in Milburngate and another in Framwellgate as 'it was a great hardship and a danger to many men returning from the collieries in the early hours of the morning'.

In 1849 the Board of Health had considered the cost of lighting the streets, since it paid a fixed annual cost to the Gas Company (founded in 1824) for the lamps and gas supplied to them. It felt that the price it paid was too high and entered negotiations to reduce it. The Board, having considered the propriety of establishing a new Gas Company and investigated the 'rights alleged to have been acquired by the City of Durham Gas Company by Twenty years possession of the Streets with their Gas Pipes' eventually backed down and renewed the contract for the lighting of the streets. The Water Company, formed in 1847, drew water from the Wear above Shincliffe Bridge. The water was filtered and then pumped up to Mountjoy Reservoir, whence it was delivered to the town by mains which had fire plugs inserted every one hundred yards. Previously the supply of water had been a problem in the summer months, for many wells and pumps ran dry. Because the river water around the peninsula was only fit for washing, drinking water had to be brought from some distance. This was in spite of the water supply to the pant in the Market Place from the Framwell.

The Nuisance Committee not only dealt with foul sewers, cesspools, ash pits and piggeries, but also in 1862 recommended that a urinal be removed from Henry Fenwick's property to near the theatre in Moatside Lane. Closely allied was the Sewerage, Paving, Lighting and Road Committee which in 1861 recommended that the Surveyor (Mr Ground) employ enough men to keep the pavements clean. There are times when Mr Ground must have felt like tearing his hair out, for not only was he charged with keeping the pavements clean, but he also had supplies of whinstone (by the hundred tons) and a tar boiler for mending roads, regularly inspected ash pits, privies, cess pools, etc to make sure that they were not in a foul state, and he was required in 1849 to inspect and repair all the pavements in the town and to lay Yorkshire Flags on a short part of the North side of Claypath as an experiment. Similar stone has recently been used for paving the Market Place, Silver Street, Framwellgate Bridge and the west side of Milburngate. Careful inspection will reveal that today's Yorkshire Flags are second hand, having been first used as tombstones in a distant Yorkshire churchyard.

While the Water Company put in fire plugs every hundred yards in its mains, the Board of Health employed the firemen in the Brigade on the basis of 1s 6d for the first house and 1s for every subsequent house in 1855. The year before, the Clerk to the Board of Health (William Marshall, Solicitor) had ordered four additional lengths of hose, each ten yards long of 'improved Copper Rivetted Leather Hose for a fire engine with Gunmetal Swivel Screws fitted to the same . . .'.

The Board of Health was the precursor of the present District Council and had itself taken over many of the functions of the earlier Corporation and parishes. The fire brigade could certainly not have survived on the 1674 gift of John Heslop to St Nicholas Parish of a ladder with 31 rungs which was to be used solely for fires 'and persons . . . borrowing the ladder to make it good upon return thereof if anything therof shall be thereby broken'. The following year the ladder was chained to the wall of the church with a lock and key!

LEFT: East and RIGHT: west end of the chapel of St Mary Magdalene.
(PAGC) BELOW: Durham County Hospital.

PART II.

GENERAL RULES.

CLEANLINESS, and HEALTH, DIET, and CLOTHING, BEDDING, &c., and SPIRITUOUS LIQUORS.

4 Geo. IV. cap. 64. Sect. 10. Rule 19.

The walls and ceilings of the wards, cells, rooms, and passages, used by the Prisoners, shall throughout be scraped and lime washed, after the gaol deliveries in every year; and also in the week next after that in which the Michaelmas, and Ephinany Sessions, shall have been held; the Prisoners shall be employed in the work.

One or more Prisoners, shall be appointed to sweep every room, and ward, in the Prison, every day; the Prisoners, shall sweep their sleeping cells daily; and all the rooms, wards, sleeping cells, and passages, shall be well and sufficiently washed once every week, from Michaelmas, to Lady-day, and twice in every week from Lady-day, to Michaelmas, and oftener, if requisite.

When the Prisoners leave their sleeping cells in the morning, the windows and doors of the cells shall be opened, nad the bed cloaths be hung up and duly aired.

Sect 10. Rule 19.

Every Prisoner before going to Chapel in the morning, shall wash his hands and face, and comb his hair; nor shall any Prisoner receive his breakfast, until he has so cleaned himself. Convenient places for the Prisoners to wash themselves, shall be provided in each ward, with an adequate allowance of soap, towels, and combs.

Sect. 10. Rule 18.

Every Prisoner shall be provided with suitable bedding, and once a week with clean body linen; and every male Prisoner with a seperate bed, hammock, or cot, either in a seperate cell, or in a cell with not less than two other male Prisoners; their blankets and rugs shall be cleaned in the week after every Quarter Sessions.

Sect 10. Rule. 20.

All Prisoners, shall be allowed as much air and exercise, as may be deemed proper for the preservation of their health.

OPPOSITE LEFT: Dean Weldon and some 'gypsies' at a Hospital Bazaar at Neville Court, 1929. (JLM)
RIGHT: North Gate when still used as a prison; Joseph Bouet, 1824. CENTRE: The new Courts and Gaol
buildings in Old Elvet; Joseph Bouet, 1824. (Both DC Add MS 95) BELOW: Rules for the Government
of Durham Gaol and House of Correction, 1824. ABOVE LEFT: Durham County Penitentiary, Gilesgate,
1871. RIGHT: The Penitentiary today is used as part of the University's accommodation and is called
Kepier House. (PAGC) BELOW LEFT: Order to George Gleason to clean up his midden and privy,
12/10/1853. (DCRO Du3/3/4: DCC) RIGHT: The Market Place in 1824, Joseph Bouet. (DC Add MS 95)
The Pant was the subject of a competition to design a replacement c1863.

LEFT: Boy being birched. (MS in DC Hunter 100 f44v; photo DUAD)
BELOW: Cosin's Grammar School on Palace Green (with his almshouses
depicted on the opposite side), Joseph Bouet, 1824. (DC Add MS 95)
RIGHT: Durham School in 1926. (DUAD)

When We Were Young

Education in Durham City goes back well into the middle ages, for the Convent had both a novice school and a song school. In the former, novices were taught in the cloister by the novice master, one of the most able of the monks. The most promising of them were creamed off and went to Durham College in Oxford University (founded by the monastery c1286). The College was a small one, consisting of eight fellows, one of whom was the warden. All were monks. Later, eight secular fellows were added. There they were trained and educated as an élite. Thomas Farne, instituted vicar of St Oswald's in 1498, had immediate permission for seven years' non-residence so that he might study at University: this must have been the medieval equivalent of a maintenance grant. In the early days of the College, students were supported by pensions, contributions and gifts from Durham Priory and its cells. In the late 14th century Bishop Hatfield and Prior Robert Berrington of Walworth jointly provided for the permanent endowment of the College. Both the novice school and the College came to an end with the Dissolution of the monastery. Some of the buildings at Durham College were, in fact, re-used in Trinity College, Oxford, when that was founded in 1555-6. Oxford's Balliol College was founded as a hostel for 16 poor scholars by John de Balliol in 1266 — an act of penance for ambushing the Bishop in 1255.

The song school for the choristers was run by the Convent's cantor from at least 1430 until the Dissolution, and then by the organist of the Cathedral. The school is still in being as the Cathedral's Chorister School, now in the College but formerly in the Sacrist's Exchequer and elsewhere in the conventual buildings. The Convent had another school for poor children, the Almoner's School, outside the Abbey Gate. It was established in the mid-14th century and came to an end at the Dissolution. It is worth remembering that the Master of the School had to celebrate Mass at the Hospital of St Mary Magdalene twice a week in the 15th and 16th centuries.

These were not the only medieval schools, for Bishop Langley founded two in 1414, one as a song school and the other for the teaching of grammar. Both were refounded by Henry VIII when the master of the Almoner's School became the assistant master of the grammar school. The two were on the east side of Palace Green from 1414. In 1640 they suffered the fate of so many public buildings; they were burnt by the Scots army. In 1661 a new school house was erected and in 1665 Bishop Cosin built his Almshouses with a school room at either end on the site of the earlier school. These rooms were used by the grammar school. The song school early lapsed into a preparatory for the grammar school and came to an end in about 1690. The post of master still continued as a sinecure for some time after. In 1844 what is now Durham School was moved off the peninsula by the Dean and Chapter to Quarryheads Lane where it remains. Its buildings and reputation have expanded steadily ever since.

Eighteenth and early nineteenth century schools were founded as charitable institutions, as adjuncts to one or other of the churches, or as private (dame) schools. The earliest is that in

Lady Ratcliffe's house in Old Elvet, where her domestic chaplain taught a school for young Catholic ladies between 1706 and 1730. There is also a single reference to a school taught by a Mr Rosse in the 1690s. In 1701 John Cock, Vicar of St Oswald's, died and left £600 to the Parish to be invested in land and property, the proceeds from which were to be used for various charitable purposes, chief among them to teach the daughters of the poor to read, spin, knit and sew. The sons of the poor were to be taught to read, write and cast accounts. By 1857 a schoolmistress taught a dozen girls and a schoolmaster two dozen boys. Both teachers also kept a Sunday School. The descendant of that school is still there today in Church Street, almost opposite the church.

According to Bishop Chandler's Visitation Returns of 1732 in St Nicholas Parish, there was '. . . one Glenn, A Quaker, . . . [with] a great many scholars both of his own persuasion and others. He teaches Latin, and I think pretends to Greek; does not much trouble himself about their coming to church'.

The Blue Coat School was founded using the charitable funds of the City in 1708 for six boys alone. Six girls were added in 1736. This educational charity was a popular one and received a number of gifts and bequests, which allowed the number of children taught and clothed to be increased. By 1802 there were sixty pupils equally divided between the sexes. St Nicholas's Sunday Schools were joined to the Blue Coat School in 1810. Two years later, the United Schools moved out of the two upper rooms in New Place, their home since 1718, and into a newly built school on the south side of Claypath. Bishop Barrington characteristically paid £309 17 0d for the land on which the school was built. It consisted of two large rooms, one above the other and two smaller rooms, the former pair used for teaching on Dr Bell's Madras System. The Master's house, however, had been converted for use by the infants' school by 1855. Numbers rose quickly after the new school had been built, for there were 207 boys and 100 girls, of whom fifty of each sex were clothed by the charity, by 1826. Twenty five years later there were also a hundred in the infants' class. It was at this point that a third, Infants' teacher was appointed.

Today it is considered that a teacher cannot impart knowledge effectively to a class greater than about thirty. Imagine the difficulties with a class of one or even two hundred! Dr Bell's system of teaching, widely adopted in the Diocese, depended on the teacher coaching selected pupils in the day's lessons either before or after school hours. Each of them would then transfer their knowledge to others in the class. Dr Bell, for a time Master of Sherburn House, advocated the use of the sandbox for teaching letters so that valuable materials might not be wasted. The sandbox was later replaced by the slate and pencil. By the 1840s this system was being replaced by older and more able pupils as teachers. After five years as a pupil teacher, such children might then proceed to a Training College, such as the Diocesan Training School at Pelaw Leazes and become a Certificated Teacher.

There was a multitude of schools in Durham during the 19th century. They were normally small establishments, only surviving as long as the founder chose to continue the establishment. In some instances children followed their parents in running the schools. George Goundy, for example, had a day school at 12 Claypath from 1851-4 and then his son taught the school until about 1868. Thomas Clarkson then used the premises as a school from 1869. This is not the only instance of a school begin apparently taken over by a new proprietor. Charles MacNally moved his school from 41 Claypath to Chapel Passage in Old Elvet, taking over a building previously used by James Bradbury. The school moved again in 1861 to Allergate.

The number of these small schools fluctuated from year to year. Before 1870 there were generally between twenty-five and thirty, which steadily declined to between fifteen and twenty over the next thirty years. Since 1905 there has been a slow decline. The long history of some of them is exemplified by the Preparatory School started by the Misses Wharton in 1865 at 6 North Bailey. It was taken over by J. H. Castley in 1898 when the school moved to 9 North Bailey. Five years later new premises were taken in Princes Street when the school became known as the Bailey School. James Hall established a boys' boarding school at 12 Leazes Lane in 1861 which became known as the Old Elvet School when it moved to 56 Old Elvet in 1869. The school eventually closed in 1905. In 1885 W. H. Bramwell established the Bow School which, of course, is still present in Durham in South Road.

There were other, larger, schools in Durham which were intended primarily for the children of the poor. The Diocesan School Society was particularly active in this field, founding three infants' schools (Church Street, Framwellgate and Claypath, actually in Gilesgate) between 1824 and 1840. Two National Schools were established in Church Street (before 1846) and in Crossgate (1861-5). While these schools were solely concerned with teaching children reading, writing and arithmetic, the Ragged School in the Clock Mill at Millburngate, formed in 1806, had rather different aims. These were 'to relieve the public from juvenile vagrancy, mendicancy and consequent depravity; to rescue as many children as possible from degradation and misery, and prepare them for a useful and respectable course of life; to try the power of kindness over the young and destitute; and thus discharge a Christian duty towards a class which particularly requires attention and amelioration'. There were 65 children on the books in 1870 of whom two thirds regularly attended. Two Board Infants' Schools were established at Gilesgate (1849) and at 106-7 Framwellgate (1888).

A major educational institution from the latter 18th century was the Sunday School and later, the schools established by the churches. The Sunday Schools provided basic education for huge numbers of children and, in the case of the various branches of Methodism, certainly many adults learnt to read, write and express themselves with clarity in public. The Wesleyan Methodists had a school at 78 New Elvet from before 1846 until 1889. Parochial schools were established by each of the three parishes other than St Nicholas, which already had the Blue Coat School.

St Margaret's School was formed in 1861. Many of the children who ought to have been going to the new school were, in fact, attending the Blue Coat School. However, by the end of that year there were 192 children: 117 boys in an upper room and 75 girls in a lower room, each taught by one teacher. By 1888 there were 239 boys and 161 girls, still taught by a master and mistress and still in two rooms. The school was difficult to heat but it is said that in winter the children were packed so closely together that they kept warm. Until 1900 the master and mistress were dependent on the services of monitors, paid 2s 6d each week, and pupil teachers, £15 per annum. They had to receive their own instruction beforehand: 8-9am and 5-7pm, occasionally in dinner hours and in the girls' school in the summer months from 6.30-9am. All of this was crucial to the survival of the school for, while each child attending paid 1d-4d for their schooling, the main funding came from a central grant of 5s 4d for each child who passed the HMI's examination in October or November each year.

The major educational institution in Durham was, and is, the University. The first attempt to found a university in Durham in the 1650s very nearly succeeded. It started in 1650 with a proposal to establish a college, school or academy for religious education to serve the north. It would be housed in the then sequestered prebendal houses in The College. Cromwell approved the proposal in 1651. Five years later, a committee reported to Cromwell's Privy Council that it also approved. The Council ordered the appointment of Trustees and vested the prebendal houses in the new college as well as various revenues of the Chapter.

Letters Patent for the establishment of the College were issued on 15 May 1657 and contained details of endowment and general organisation to be known as 'the Provost, Fellows and Scholars of the College in Durham of the Foundation of Oliver, Lord Protector'. The College seems to have become established, but in 1658 controversy reared its head. The College had made an attempt to achieve University status and Letters Patent. On the Restoration a year later, it was dismantled.

About one hundred and seventy years after the closure of the first College, a new one was mooted. Pressure for Parliamentary Reform in the early nineteenth century was accompanied by no little pressure for ecclesiastical reform, not ameliorated by the Bishops' opposition to the Reform Bill in 1831. In that year Bishop Van Mildert and Canon Thorp found an answer to the major complaint against the clergy, that they, both in general and in Durham, had more revenue than was necessary for their work. Van Mildert and Thorp proposed that the excess revenue be used to endow a northern college. Within two months of the original proposal the College had grown to a University and, more important, the Dean and all the members of the Chapter had been persuaded to support the proposal. On 4 July 1832 the University of Durham Act became law and the first undergraduates were admitted for the Michaelmas Term.

The University started life in Archdeacon's Inn (later Cosin's Hall) and was totally controlled by the Dean and Chapter. There was a broad curriculum in the Arts to which Engineering was added in 1838 (the first such course in the country, though unfortunately short-lived). By 1862 the University had degenerated into little more than a theological college with a mere 42 students. Following a measure of reform, the University grew and eventually the hold of the Dean and Chapter was completely removed by the University of Durham Act 1908. Over the years the University had come to be associated with the School of Medicine and Armstrong College in Newcastle. The 1908 Act recognised this and formalised the relationship between the three parts of the University. The Newcastle division seems always to have been larger than that of Durham, and became the University of Newcastle in 1963.

Various originally independent educational institutions have been drawn into the University. The two Diocesan teacher training colleges of St Hild (founded 1858) and St Bede (founded 1839) were early drawn into association and ultimately offered University degrees (1896 and 1892 respectively). The other teachers' training college at Neville's Cross (founded 1922) was drawn into association but that connection has recently been dissolved as the college has been amalgamated with the Framwellgate Moor Technical College under the title of New College. Two of the University's Colleges started life as independent theological colleges, later to be incorporated in the University in 1923. St Chads was founded at Hooton Pagnall in 1902 and moved to Durham in 1904. St John's was founded in 1909 as a branch of St John's College, Highbury.

The University already had three other colleges. University College was first housed in Archdeacon's Inn and, once the keep had been rebuilt by Salvin in 1840, later moved to the Castle. More recently the accommodation of the College has been expanded by the construction of a new building between Moatside Lane and Saddler Street. Hatfield Hall, later to become a College, was established in 1846 in the North Bailey. It was intended that those students who could not afford the high life of University College (which for a time included a beagle pack among its assets) could be accommodated here. The College grew quickly and has been enlarged several times since 1846. There was a short-lived attempt to use Archdeacon's Inn as a residence known as Cosin's Hall (1851-64). The building, now used to house students from University College, still bears the name given to it in 1851.

Women were first admitted to study for degrees in 1895. Until 1899 they either stayed at home or with relations, since the University made no provision for them. In 1899 the University obtained 33 Claypath for their accommodation. Later they moved to Abbey House and then one of the prebendal houses in The College. Eventually it was possible to build St Mary's College (as the Women's Hostel became known in 1920) on its present site between 1947-51. A new block was opened in 1962. Other colleges have been formed since then and built on the slope facing the south side of the town and Cathedral. These include Collingwood College (1971-3), Grey College (1960) Trevelyan College (1964-7) Van Mildert College (1962-6) and St Aidan's College (buildings erected 1962-4) which began life as a Society for home students in 1946 and became a formally constituted College of the University in 1961.

ABOVE: Johnson Technical School (now moved to Crossgate Moor and the school replaced by houses). (DUAD) LEFT: The Charter of the Cromwellian University; (DPAD: PK) RIGHT: detail of Cosin's Hall showing the doorway, 1883.

127

LEFT: Bede College, the Diocesan Teacher Training College for men.
RIGHT: St Chad's College, South Bailey, 1956. BELOW: Rear of St
John's College, 1956.

128

LEFT: St John's College, South Bailey, 1956. RIGHT: Hatfield College,
c1950. BELOW: Terrace walk of St John's College, 1956. (All DUAD)

ABOVE: DLI Chapel in the Cathedral. (DC) BELOW: Rowing has been a strong sport in Durham since before the first Regatta in 1834. 1984 (photo) saw the 150th Anniversary of that first Regatta, with crews drawn from the University Colleges, the City Club, and Durham School as well as much further afield. (AC)

Yesterday, Today and then Today

Many aspects of Durham's past have been touched on in the foregoing pages. Many others have been omitted for want of space. Durham today is not, like the New Towns at Washington, Newton Aycliffe or Peterlee, a brand new creation straight off the architect's drawing board. It is the product of almost a millenium of change and growth. Bishop, Prior and King have all played a part in influencing the layout of the various parts and it is on these early outlines that the ordinary man has added the flesh of buildings of one sort or another. Very few of these survive, for the greater part are now merely ghosts to be detected in archaeological deposits. The few that do survive, together with the principal buildings erected by those in power, all show that time has not passed them by unheeding, for each generation has both added to and taken away from its inheritance. We will never again see a new Cathedral or Castle, for the time of erecting such buildings on that scale in Durham has gone. Certainly it is difficult to envisage a new building to equal the best in the world, as Durham Cathedral has recently been so declared.

New buildings have risen, are now rising and will rise on the sites of earlier ones. It is a tribute to the present Council and its immediate predecessor that Durham is one of only five demonstration towns in the United Kingdom in the Council of Europe's Campaign for Urban Renewal. One problem that has exercised the Council for over a century has been the volume of traffic in the City centre. As early as the 1880s a relief road coupled with a new bridge over the Wear was proposed. This was repeated in 1930 and the plan carried to the point of execution, but not executed. In 1944 Sharp's plan for the City developed that plan together with others for the renewal of the more derelict areas of the town. The oldest part of the plan, the relief road and new bridge over the Wear, was modified to include a second new bridge at Elvet, so that it was possible to keep nearly all traffic out of the centre. Framwellgate and Elvet Bridges were then closed to vehicles and they, together with the Market Place, were resurfaced and made into an integral pedestrian precinct with limited access for traffic. It is this development, concerned with relieving the City centre of traffic, as well as the redevelopment of the derelict areas of Elvet Riverside and the area north of Framwellgate Bridge (Millburngate Shopping Centre), that has lifted Durham to the forefront in urban renewal and was so recognised in the issue of postage stamps in April 1984.

Just as many buildings have gone, so some of Durham's institutions have gone too. One in particular has carried the name of City and County all over the world with pride and gained no little glory in the process. The Durham Light Infantry, so named only in 1808, was first raised in 1758 as Lambton's Regiment of Foot, the 68th Regiment in the line. It was renamed the Durham Regiment of Foot in 1782. In 1873 the 106th Bombay Light Infantry (formerly the East India Company's 2nd Bombay European Light Infantry, raised in 1840) became the 2nd Battalion of the DLI. The two militia and five Volunteer Battalions brought the Regiment's strength to nine battalions. In the course of the Great War, a further twenty eight battalions were raised. The equivalent of twelve battalions never returned.

In the course of the Second World War fewer battalions were raised, and several of those became specialists. The 2nd Battalion was destroyed in the retreat to Dunkirk in 1940. It was subsequently re-raised and saw distinguished service in the Far East in 1944-5. After the War, the strength of the Regiment was reduced to one Regular (1st) battalion and two Territorial (6th and 8th) battalions. They and representatives of the 437th and 463rd Regiments and the 17th Parachute Battalion, which had originally been DLI battalions, were present at Brancepeth Castle (the Regiment's Depôt from 1939) in 1958 to celebrate the completion of the Regiment's second century of existence.

The DLI ceased to be a county-based Regiment in 1968, when it was absorbed into the Light Infantry. One of the most attractive museums in the north was erected in 1968, in the grounds of County Hall at Aykley Heads, to record and preserve for all time the magnificent history of the DLI. More sombre memorials are the Chapel in the Cathedral and the DLI garden on the south side of the claustral buildings.

In conflict of a less lethal nature Durham takes pride in her Regatta, established in 1834, and thus the oldest established in the country. The Cricket Club was founded a century ago in 1884, while The Wasps, Durham's more recently established ice-hockey team, is well-known and successful in national competition. The ancient sport of golf was established on a course at Mount Oswald in 1887 and the house, built in 1830, now serves as the Club house. One long-established sport that, alas, no longer survives in the City, is horse racing. In the mid-17th century we find individuals providing prizes either of plate or purses for flat races in Durham. These were run on the Smyddyhaughs where the University now has playing fields. It was, in fact, the University which caused the races to come to an end in 1887, when it refused to renew the Race Course lease.

Football is, of course, an ancient sport which has been played by many groups and clubs at all levels. The earliest reference to an organised match is in the latter part of the 17th century when a tanner's apprentice took the afternoon off (without leave) to represent the Tanners in a match against apprentices of another craft. Durham City now has its own team, playing on a ground called Ferens Park, after Alderman Ferens, who greatly assisted the club in the 1930s.

The buildings, institutions, clubs, pubs and parks that we know in Durham today are the product of discussion and argument, action and reaction, sometimes lasting a week, occasionally over centuries. Durham City is the scene of a battle between past and present which the present fleetingly wins until it, too, becomes the past. The town that is here today will have changed in a century's time. Today's decisions are tomorrow's monuments, memories and photographs.

ABOVE: View west from the foot of Claypath with the Palace Cinema on the left (formerly Henderson's Dye house) and Hugh MacKay's carpet factory on the right, before 1960. BELOW: Framwellgate Peth from the foot of Claypath before the advent of the National Savings building. (Both JMB)

Yesterday's Silver Street from John Duck's House, (TM) and
OPPOSITE: The Fulling Mill, nestling at the foot of the Cathedral, has
had a chequered career. Most recently it was the University's
Department of Archaeology, but in 1975 it became the Museum of
Archaeology — home to much of what survives of the City's past. (DC)

Select Bibliography

M. Abernethy: *A history of the church of St Nicholas, Durham,* Durham, 1981.

W. Ainsley: *Historical and Descriptive Sketches of the City of Durham and its environs* Durham 1849.

C. A. Alington: *Durham Cathedral: the story of a thousand years* Durham 1949.

G. Allan: *Historical and Descriptive View of the City of Durham* (includes R. Hegge's *Legend of St Cuthbert* as an Appendix) Durham 1824.

T. Allom and T. Rose: *Westmorland, Cumberland, Durham and Northumberland Illustrated.* London 1832.

Anon: *St Margaret's School, 1861-1961* Durham 1961.

  The Church of Our Lady of Mercy and St Godric. Durham 1964.

T. Arnold (ed): *Symeonis Monachi Opera* Rolls Series ii 1885.

J. Barmby (ed): *Vestry Books of Parish Churches of Durham City* Surtees Society 84 (1888).

  Memorials of St Giles Surtees Soc, vol 95 (1896).

C. F. Battiscombe (ed): *The relics of St Cuthbert* London 1956.

R. W. Billings: *Architectural Illustration and Description of the Cathedral Church at Durham.* London, 1843.

H. Bowen-Jones & W. Fisher: *Durham City.* Durham 1972.

J. R. Boyle: *Guide to Durham* Durham 1892.

E. J. Burrow: *About and around Durham.* c1920.

B. Callender: *Education in the Melting Pot* Norwich 1972.

M. O. H. Carver: *Excavations in New Elvet, Durham City 1961-73, Arch. Aeliana* 5th ser, 2(1974) 91-148.

  Three Saxo-Norman Tenements in Durham City *Med Arch* 23(1979) 1-80.

P. A. G. Clack & P. F. Gosling: *Archaeology in the North,* Durham 1976.

J. Clipson: Back Silver Street, Durham 1975-6 Excavations. *Arch Aeliana,* 5th Ser. 8(1980) 109-126.

N. Coldstream & P. Draper (eds): *Medieval Art and Architecture in Durham Cathedral* B.A.A., London 1980.

B. Colgrave & R. C. Norris: *St Margaret's Church, Crossgate, Durham* Durham 1973.

S. Coll: Structural *Analysis of the . . . Gardener's Store in the Cathedral Yard, Durham.* Unpub B. A. Diss, Dept Arch, Durham Univ. 1979.

R. J. Cramp: *A Corpus of Anglo-Saxon Sculpture: Northumberland and Durham* London 1983.

R. E. G. Cranfield: *100 Years of Prisoners Aid in County Durham. 1882-1982* Durham, 1982.

H. Derbyshire: *A history of the Congregational church, Durham.* Durham, 1933.

J. W. Dickenson: *Disease, Death and Dotage in Durham* Unpub MS, D. City Library, c1975.

R. B. Dobson: *Durham Priory 1400-1450* London 1973.

M. H. Dodds: The Bishop's Boroughs *Arch. Aeliana,* 3rd ser, 12(1915) 81-185.

R. H. Edleston & C. W. Gibby: Grave Covers at St Oswald's, Durham *Trans D. & N.* 1st ser 10(1954) 130-6.

N. Emery: *St John Boste and the Waterhouse,* Durham, 1982.

W. Fordyce: *The History and Antiquities of the County Palatine of Durham.* Newcastle 1857.

J. T. Fowler (ed): *Rites of Durham* Surtees Society vol 107(1902).

  Durham University London, 1904.

C. M. Fraser (ed): *Records of Anthony Bek* Surtees Society vol 162 (1947).

  A History of Antony Bek. London 1957.

  Northern Petitions Surtees Society vol 194 (1981).

C. W. Gibby: A note on the church of St Mary the Less, Durham *Trans D & N,* 1st ser, 10(1954) 245-250.

  Durham Freeman and the Guilds Durham 1971.

P. A. Grant: *The Coalmines of Durham City* Dept Geography, D.U., Occ Papers No 2; 1973.

W. Greenwell (ed): *Bishop Hatfield's Survey.* Surtees Society vol 32(1856).

  Durham Cathedral 9th Ed. Durham, 1932.

  Foedarium Prioratus Dunelmensis Surtees Society vol 58 (1871).

Sir T. D. Hardy (ed): *Registrum Palatinum Dunelmensis* 4 vols London 1877-8.

F. J. Haverfield & W. Greenwell: *A Catalogue of the sculptured and inscribed stones in the Cathedral Library, Durham* Durham 1899.

F. H. Hawkins *History of the Presbytery of Durham* South Shields 1976.

A. Heeson: *The founding of the University of Durham,* Durham 1982.

G. Hinde (ed): *The Registers of Bishops Tunstall and Pilkington* Surtees Society vol 161 (1852).

M. Hird (ed): *St Mary's College 1899-1974.* Durham 1976.

M. P. Howden (ed): *The Register of Bishop Fox* Surtees Society vol 147 (1932).

W. Hutchinson: *The History and Antiquities of the County Palatine of Durham,* vol II (1787).

F. F. Johnson: *Historic Staircases in Durham City.* Durham 1970.

M. Johnson: The North East Altar in the Galilee of Durham Cathedral, *Trans D & N,* 1st ser, 11 (1958-65) 371-90.

W. T. Jones: The Walls and Towers of Durham *Durham Univ J* 22-23, 6 parts.

E. Kitzinger: *The Coffin of St Cuthbert* Oxford, 1950.

E. Mackenzie & M. Ross: *An Historical, topographical and descriptive view of the County Palatine of Durham* Newcastle 1834.

D. M. Meade: The Hospital of St Giles at Kepier, Near Durham, *Trans D & N*, 2nd ser 1(1970), 45-55.

G. H. Metcalfe *A History of the Durham Miners Association 1869-1915,* Unpub MS, DUL, Durham University. 1947.

I. Nelson: *Durham as it was.* Nelson, Lancs, 1974.

H. S. Offler (ed): *Durham Episcopal Charters* Surtees Society 179 (1966).

L. Olsover: *The Jewish Communities of North East England* Newcastle, 1981.

G. Ormsby: *Sketches of Durham.* Durham 1846.

W. Page (ed): *The Victoria County History of Durham* 3 vols. London, 1905-28.

L. Pennington: *An account of Durham.* Durham, 1804.

N. Pevsner & E. Williamson: *The Buildings of England: County Durham* 2nd ed. London, 1983.

D. Pocock & R. Gazzard: *Durham: Portrait of a Cathedral City* Durham 1983.

J. Raine: *Saint Cuthbert with an account of the state in which his remains were found upon opening his tomb in Durham Cathedral in the year 1827.* Durham 1828.

    A Brief Account of Durham Cathedral Newcastle 1833.

    Historiae Dunelmensis: scriptores tres Surtees Society, vol (1839).

R. S. Robson, *Presbyterian church, Durham,* Durham 1922.

G. V. Scammell: *Hugh du Puiset* London 1954.

T. Sharp: *Cathedral City: a plan for Durham,* Durham 1944.

M. G. Snape: *Durham City*: lecture given to Soc Ants Newcastle. 1976.

J. W. Steel: *Early Friends in the North* 1905.

R. L. Storey (ed): *Bishop Langleys Registers* Surtees Society vols 164,166,169,170,177,182 (1949-1967).

    Thomas Langley and the Bishopric of Durham. London, 1961.

R. Surtees: *The History and Antiquities of the County Palatine of Durham,* 4 vols, Durham 1816-1840.

F. Thompson: The church of St Giles *Trans D & N* 1st ser 1(1862-8) 129-133.

    St Mary Magdalene, *Trans D & N,* 1st ser 2(1869-79) 140-46).

W. Thwaites: *Wesleyan Methodism in Durham City* Durham, 1909.

L. Toulmin Smith (ed): *The Itinerary of John Leland in or about the years 1535-1543.*

J. M. Tweedy: *Popish Elvet* 2 vols, Durham 1981-4.

G. Walker: *A Brief sketch of Durham for the use of visitors and others.* Durham, 1870.

S. G. P. Ward: *Faithful: the story of the DLI* London 1963.

C. E. Whiting: *The Unversity of Durham, 1832-1932* Durham 1932.

    Durham Civic Memorials Surtees Society vol 160 (1952).

T. A. Whitworth: *Yellow Sandstone and Mellow Brick* Durham 1972.

T. E. Yates: *A College Remembered* Durham 1981.

In addition to the usual PRO Calenders, the *Reports of the Deputy Keeper of the Public Records* are invaluable. The relevant Reports are numbers 16(1855), 29(1868), 30(1869), 31(1870), 32(1871), 33(1872), 35(1875), 37(1876), 44(1883) and 45(1884).

Manuscript sources are numberless, but the following have been particularly useful: in the Dean and Chapter Library, the Romans, Longstaffe, Sharpe and Hunter MSS; in the Department of Palaeography and Diplomatic, the Baker Papers and the Episcopal Visitation returns; in the County Record Office, the papers of the Local Board of Health and the collections of materials relating to the Methodist, Baptist and Congregational Churches. In the Northumberland Room of Newcastle Central Library there is an invaluable series of bound *Local Tracts*.

Key to Caption Credits

AC	Mr A. Clark
AHR	Mr A. H. Reed
ARM	Mr A. R. Middleton
DC	Dean and Chapter Library
DCC	Durham City Council
DCRO	Durham County Record Office
DPAD,PK	Department of Palaeography and Diplomatic, Durham University, Prior's Kitchen
DUAD	Department of Archaeology, Durham University
DUL	Durham University Library
HM	Hugh MacKay Ltd
JGA	J. & G. Archibald Ltd
JLM	Mr J. L. Myres
JMB	Mr & Mrs J. M. Balfour
NEAU	Archaeological Unit for North East England
PAGC	Peter Clack
TM	Mr T. Middlemass
TW	Mr T. Woods

Index

140

Subscribers

Presentation Copies

1 Durham City Council
2 Durham County Council
3 The Dean & Chapter Library, Durham Cathedral
4 The Dept of Palaeography & Diplomatic
5 Durham University Library
6 Durham University, Dept of Archaeology
7 Durham County Record Office
8 Cllr Alan Crooks JP

9 Peter & Heather Clack
10 Clive & Carolyn Birch
11 The Right Worshipful The Mayor of Durham
12 R.J.B. Morris
13
23 The City of Durham
24 The City of Durham Council
25 Edison G. Clack
26 Victoria May Clack
27 M.D. Clack
28 Elaine McCreath
29 H.A. Johnson
30 Frederick Riseborough
31 Grace Turnbull
32 Cleveland County
46 Library
47 Lloyd J. Edwards
48 Dr & Mrs C.D. Watkinson
49 St Pauls Jarrow Development Trust
50 University of Durham
51 Ada Radford
52 J.P. Allatt
53 Chetham's Library, Manchester
54 Ushaw Moor County Junior School
55 Margaret I. Peel
56 J.L. Myers & Son Ltd
57
58 E.D. Howard
59 South Tyneside Central Library
60 Faith Dodd
61 Roland Bibby
62 Durham County
111 Library
112 C.D. Morris
113 S.J. Dodd

114 Jean M. Seddon
115 Patricia Rennison
116 Mrs Grace McCombie
117 Dr P.M. Hacking
118 E.B. Phillips
119 City of Newcastle
121 Upon Tyne Libraries Dept
122 A.M.M. Clayden
123 Dr D.W. Watson
124 James Milligan
125 June Crosby
126 Iain Grant Mitchell
127 A.K. Lamballe
128 N.M. Teesdale
129 Dr J.C. Yule
130 J. & C. Archibald
131 Chris Clarke
132
133 J.C. Bartle
134 N.T. Hart
135 J. Bowron
136 Avril Williamson
137 James Derrick Storey
138 J. Gott
139
140 R.J. Dickinson
141 A.F. Coulson
142 David Armstrong
143 Murray & Jessie Balfour
144 Mrs A.E. Perkins
145 Dr I.H. Taylor
146 Mrs O.H. Batey
147 E.E. Carlin
148 Allan Ramsden
149 K. Swales
150 D. Bowman
151 Ian B. Mackay
152 C.M. Hulbert
153 Lawrence Embleton
154 M.J.G. Barber
155 Penelope Wilson
156 G.J. Waughman
157 Eric W. Hall
158 N.J. Till

159 W.B. Standish
160 The Thompson Family
161
162 R.J. Dickinson
163 Dr Pamela R. Cooper
164 Mr Carter·
165
167 Mrs M.A. Shirpet
168 Mrs M. Parkinson
169 Norman Walker
170 D.R. Featonby
171 Mrs S. Stone
172 T.F. Watson
173 Ramshaw County School
174 C.D. Morris
175 Edith Kerr
176 H.G.E. Wilson
177 Dr & Mrs R.P. Tanham
178 C.F.C. Lawson
179 Frank Atkinson
180 Mrs Parkinson
181 Gerald B. Champion
182 Clive Lemmon
183 Clara Doreen Nichol
184 Ian & Pamela Forbes
185
186 Kathleen Haywood
187 E. Audrey Gilkerson
188 David Tonks
189 Eric Aylen Gordon Preston
190 Mrs Maureen Oliphant
191 Eileen Davison
192 Thomas Henry Rowland
193 J.R. Robinson
194 Dept. of Adult Education — The University of Durham
195 M.G. Snape
196 J.E. Jewitt

197 William E.J. Ricketts
198 C.W. Worswick
199 A.J. Nicholson
200 Mrs J.R. Gardner
201 E. Marshall
202 Alan Hall
203 T.R. Hornshaw
204 John Gosden
205 Anthony Richmond
206 Dr M. Overton
207 A.M. Bankier
208 K.G. Hall
209 A.J. Lilbunt
210 Joseph R. Grieves
211 Roger Norris
212 Bryan Chambers
213 Catherine J. Sinburn
214 Keith Best
215 J. Hampson
216 J.E. Colley
217 Noel & Janet Jackson
218 Mrs Diane M. Smith
219 C.J. Higgins
220 Ian Curry
221 Malcolm Urquhart
222 Canon F.S.M. Chase
223 City of Newcastle
224   upon Tyne
225 L.P. Wenham
227 Michael Bartley
228 Derek Angus Peart
229 Martin K. Jones
230
231 Dr C.M. Fraser
232 G. Harbottle
233 Nicholas Pattinson
234 M.J.M. McVitie
235 James Fairlie
236 Mrs R.R. Mawson

237
238 Miss J. Sotheran
239 D.J. Butler
240 Faye MacLeod
241 Marie-Thérèse
     Pinder
242 Don Wilcock
243 Warwick Road
     School, — Bishop
     Auckland
244 Abbey Junior School
     — Darlington
245 T.M. Heron
246 Mayor's Officer
247 P.J. Storey
248 Mrs G.N. Ivy
249 Percival Turnbull
250 John Davison
251 Mrs M.P. Lamb
252 Mrs E. Waugh
253 Mrs Ebbatson
254 Mr C. McGovern
255 Miss M. Leheup
256 V.T. Scott
257 D. Watson
258 J.R. Robson
259 Noel & Janet Jackson
260 M.T. Pinder
261
262 B.J. Hunter
263 R.J.B. Morris
264 Francis McCluskey
265 Audrey Cumming
266 John B. Scollen
267 Mrs Miles
268 H.H. Wills
269 Elemore Hall Reg
     School
270
275 J.&G. Archibald Ltd.

276 George Watson
277 Anne Gardner
278 Peter R. Causnett
279 Scott Haggart
280 Keith William Smith
281 Raymond W.R.
     Roberts
282 Miss N.J.T. Bratt
283
284 Jordison-Rook
285 Mrs E.M. Cosker
286 Mrs M.A. Smith
287 Valerie Richardson
288 R.J. Dickinson
289 Christopher
     Crawford
290 A. Gatiss
291
292 Margaret Hedley
293 Sheila McLean
294 Mrs M.J. Thorp
295 E.L. Wilson
296 Joan Trowbridge
297 Mrs I. Field
298 Stella Jackson
299 Graham G. Gardner
300 Peter Burdess
301 A.R. Middleton
302 G.W. Hancock
303 Mary Parker
304 Ronald French
305 Mrs B. Whatmore
306 John Foster
307 St. Cuthbert's R.C.
     Primary School
308 Mrs S. Richardson
309 Mrs P. Calderwood
310 Mrs M. Coulson
311 Tom Middlemass
312 Trevor Woods
Remaining names unlisted

ENDPAPERS: LEFT — Durham City c.1611; RIGHT — from Allan's
Guide to Durham, 1824.

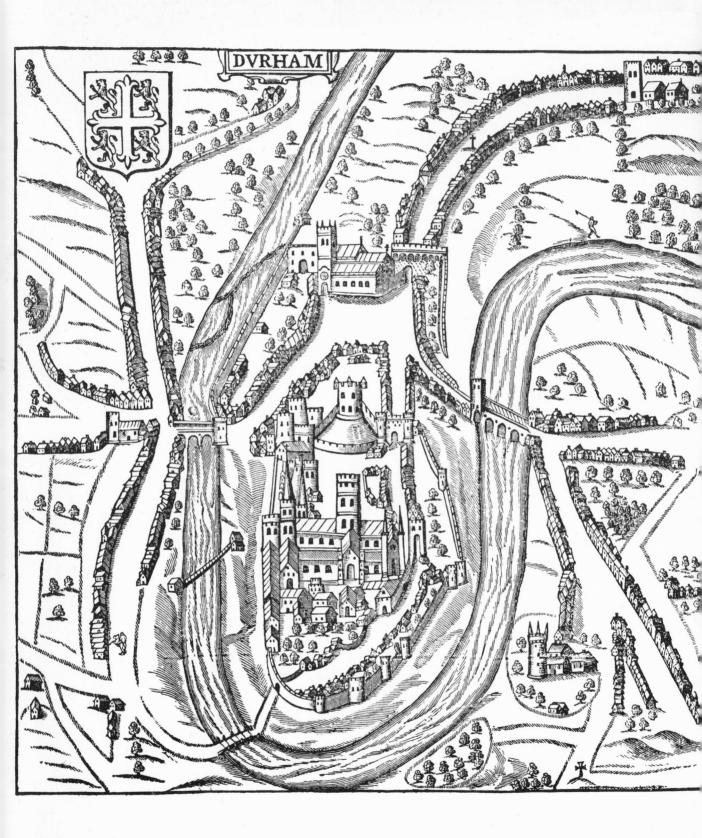